My One-Star Amazon Reviews and the Articles that Earned Them

Jane Gilgun

"To laugh, perchance to dream...."

CONTENTS

FOREWORD

I was stung a few years ago when people began to rate my articles on Amazon Kindle with one star out of five. One woman gave one-star review that consisted of a few sentences on how much her grandson loves his Kindle reader and how she was disappointed the article wasn't a children's book she could read with him. I was delighted to hear that the boy likes his Kindle because maybe he would buy the article his grandmother didn't like, which was about the sex education of children. A UK reader was angry because in my article on women's aging body parts I didn't discuss the symptoms of menopause and the information was depressing. Someone else awarded one star because I ignored the sexual abuse of boys when I did not.

I decided to make these article available as a package and see if other readers think they are as bad as these raters think. I could not reprint the reviews in this collection because of copyright issues, but I do present fair use excerpts at the beginning of each article.

I hope readers don't look for a connected set of articles. Some of them are, such as Marly's stories and the articles on executive function, on lust, agape, etc., and the sex education of children. Turtle Night at Playa Grande probably doesn't fit with other articles, but in my mind the kind of callousness so many have toward the survival of leatherback turtles is similar to the callousness of family policies toward children.

As a University professor, I teach and attempt to follow the principles of critical thinking. Even-handedness and general statements supported by evidence are among those principles. Even-handedness means we fairly represent the points of view of others. When we have alternative points of view, we support them with evidence. It's wonderful to get this kind of critique. It means readers respect the work enough to give well-founded feedback. Sadly, the one-star reviews I received did not follow these principles. Thus, they did not help me improve my articles.

Jane Gilgun
Minneapolis, Minnesota
25 August 2013

1

Executive Function
and Self-Regulation in Children

Reviewer: *"an abstract…not an actual book"*

Executive function is a term that covers a broad range of capacities related to judgment, problem-solving, organization of self, anticipation of consequences, working memory, and following rules and directions. Regulation of emotions, thoughts, and behaviors is part of executive function as well.

Five year-old Jasmine climbs onto the roof of the garage and is about to jump off because she thinks she can fly. Mario grabs an eraser off another second grader's desk because he doesn't have one. Oliver teases another child on the bus because the other child wears dirty clothes and stinks. These are examples of common executive function issues in children.

Children develop good executive functions when they feel safe and engage in reciprocal relationships of love and care. Safety is ensured when adults provide routines and structure, are clear in their expectations, recognize and praise appropriate behaviors, explain reasons for rules, and provide guidance for alternative behaviors when children behave inappropriately. Reciprocity is assured when parents are sensitive and responsive in a contingent way; that is, in ways that match children's capacities. When this happens, children are responsive in appropriate ways to their parents.

When Oliver's parents learned that he was teasing another child, they invited him for a walk in the woods and asked him whether he'd ever been teased. Oliver thought for a while and then remembered that his older brother Damien made fun of him when he told the family at dinnertime that he had a girlfriend. Oliver's parents asked him how he felt when Damien teased him. "Awful," Oliver said. "I just wanted him to stop."

Oliver's parents didn't know about the teasing. They had a long conversation about what teasing is, how it feels, and how important it is to tell parents or other adults about the teasing. Oliver spontaneously shared that he had teased another kid on the bus. With no prompting, he said, "I did what Damien did to me. I shouldn't do that." His parents said, "What a guy. Thanks for telling us. Why shouldn't you tease other kids?" "Teasing hurts," Oliver answered. He never again teased the other child. He told other kids to leave the child alone, too. Oliver responded well to his parents' concerns about teasing. Oliver had grown up in a family where parents were generally sensitive and responsive.

Children develop issues with executive function and self-regulation under three different conditions. The first is when parents are generally insensitive and non-responsive and have poor executive skills themselves. These parents do not have expectations for rule-following such as respecting others and respecting the property of others. They do not recognize when children do things well. They don't teach their children appropriate ways of expressing emotions and interacting with others.

The second is when children have neurological issues that predispose them to difficulties with executive function. I'll talk about this in more detail later, but autism spectrum issues or fetal alcohol issues are examples of conditions that children have that predispose them to trouble with executive function. These children may have sensitive, responsive, and competent parents.

A third situation where children have executive function issues is when they have both insensitive, non-responsive parents and neurological issues. Children in these situations often come to attention of social service agencies in schools and communities.

In this article, I first discuss executive function and then provide detail about self-regulation, a major component of executive function.

Neurobiological Basis of Executive Function

The neurological basis of executive function is located primarily in the prefrontal cortex, which is in the front of the brain and is the seat of reasoning. The term "executive" fits these sets of capacities because an executive is someone who is in charge. The prefrontal cortex, however, is connected to many other areas of the brain, such as emotion and motor centers.

Like brain functioning in general, executive functions or skills arise from a combination of genetics and experience. Adequate nutrition and good prenatal care as well as genetics lead to good executive functions at birth. Subsequent experience contributes further to executive function development. With sensitive, responsive care, children build upon existing skills to continue their optimal development.

Stress, trauma, abuse, and neglect may undermine the development of executive skills in children with a good genetic makeup. These children can recover or develop new executive skills if their circumstances change for the better, where parenting is sensitive and responsive.

Conversely, many children are born with brain functions that predispose them to executive function issues, but their quality of care is so high that they develop new neural circuits that appear to compensate for what might have been executive function deficits. How much neural growth is possible is related to genetic makeup and whether or not any brain damage has ceiling effects. For example, there appear to be ceiling effects for some of the executive functions of children with fetal alcohol effects.

Parents of children with executive function challenges may require emotional support and psychoeducation and the children's development of executive skills could take longer than with other children. Once again, however, there are limits to the brain's plasticity and some individuals may have life-long issues with executive functions.

Examples

Executive function issues include difficulties with attention, following directions and rules, organizing the self, self-soothing when stressed, and self-regulation, and impulse control. Impulse control and following involves capacities for holding information in working memory and in considering alternatives and consequences, as well as resistance to distractions.

Some executive function issues are primarily neurobiological in origin. They include fetal alcohol spectrum disorders, autism spectrum disorders, and attention deficit/hyperactivity disorders (ADHD). The more sensitive and attuned parents and other adults can be to children with executive functioning and neurological issues, the more likely that children will have capacities for self-regulation to the degree possible with their neurological issues.

In addition, conduct issues such as oppositional, defiant, self-harming, and antisocial behaviors could be related to trauma and to imitation of behaviors children have observed. Many children are raised in families where acting without apparent thought of possible harm to self and others is the prime means of dealing with conflict. Children in these situations have learned to believe that tantrums, violence, and destruction of property are how they are supposed to deal with upsetting situations.

Some children have neurological issues and histories of untreated trauma. These children will have issues with executive function and require special care.

What to Do

Children with executive function issues require structure in their daily lives, clear and simple directions in how to accomplish tasks, clear expectations, and praise when they show the smallest executive skill. They benefit when others show them how to do things and when the adults around them also have good executive skills.

As with other challenging child behaviors, parents of children with executive function issues benefit from psychoeducation, parent support groups, and professionals who themselves have good executive skills. Parent support groups can be especially helpful. Not only do parents learn how other parents help their children, the also learn that they are not alone. Other parents have similar difficulties with their own self-regulation when they have children who are challenging.

Psychoeducation usually takes place in groups. Parents receive information related to their children's conditions and have opportunities to talk about how to apply that information to their particular situations. Psychoeducation can not only add to stores of knowledge but can be therapeutic. Parents often feel great relief when they understand what is happening for their children and for themselves.

Parents often need time away from their children, or respite care, on a regular and as needed basis. Sometimes social services provide respite. Sometimes parents have other family members and friends who can lend a hand. Some parents may find crisis nurseries to be a solution when they feel as if they are about to dysregulate. Parents' executive functions are compromised if they have chemical dependency issues and untreated mental illness.

Practice Note

Once practitioners have reason to believe that children have executive function issues, it is advisable to assess parents' executive functions. Children learn good executive skills from their everyday experiences of care that parents and others provide. The case of six year-old Jack who has a diagnosis of ADHD will illustrate this point. Besides impulsivity and distractibility, Jack has explosive behaviors that require containment several times a day in order to keep himself and others safe. Explosive behaviors that could harm self or others are not characteristic of ADHD. They could be learned behaviors, behaviors whose origins are not known, or behaviors related to neurological conditions. A genogram showed that Jack's father was diagnosed with schizophrenia and his mother with bipolar disorder. Jack could have inherited a pre-disposition for a neurological condition characterized by issues with executive function and self-regulation. One or both parents could have explosive behaviors that threated the safety of themselves and others. Jack could have learned these behaviors from observation. He could believe these are expectable and natural responses to stress.

A thorough assessment helps practitioners to identify the contributions neurobiological issues may have and the contributions of

4

parenting styles and family life to Jack's behavioral issues. If the parents manage their conditions well, there is reason to be optimistic about Jack's long-term outcome. However, if parents' conditions are unpredictable, untreated, and unmanaged, chances are parents will be unable to provide stability and consistency of love and care that Jack requires to develop good executive and self-regulation skills. They may be unable to model self-regulation, but continue to be explosive themselves.

A thorough assessment of child and family issues will result in a treatment plan, which is a course of recommended actions to help Jack and his family. Typical parts of plans are referrals to parenting classes, parent support groups, and psychotherapy, which can be a combination of individual, family, and couple treatment. Parents may resist some or all of these recommendations on the grounds that they aren't crazy or professionals are. Service providers will be most helpful if they listen carefully to parental concerns and show the same kind of sensitivity and responsiveness that they recommend that parents have for their children.

Another important application of the concept of executive function is to assess who is in charge of the family; in other words, who has the executive functions for the family. In traditional families, where fathers and husbands are in charge of household finances and child discipline, women may struggle with executive function issues if their husbands die or leave the family. An older child may assume executive roles, but not have the skills to fulfill them.

For example, Pang, a Hmong refugee, a widow, and the mother of six children ages sixteen to six, depended upon her sixteen year-old daughter Moa to use the cash card that county social services agency provided every month. Pang did not know how to use the card and asked Moa to do it. Moa spent the money on clothes and entertainment for herself and her friends, leaving the family in serious financial difficulties, and showing her poor executive functions in this situation. An effective treatment plan would assist Pang in taking on executive functions.

Self-Regulation

Self-regulation is defined as capacities to manage and make sense of one's own thoughts, emotions, and behaviors in times of stress and in the course of everyday life. Some view self-regulation as one of the executive functions. Capacities for self regulation are both genetic and experiential in origin. Subjectively, children experience dysregulation as a loss of control, of unmanageability of thoughts, emotions, and behaviors. Heart rate and breathing may become accelerated.

When dysregulated, individuals throughout the life course may become fearful, anxious, withdrawn, depressed, hyperactive, lethargic, and experience emotional outbursts, bed wetting, sleep disturbances, and oppositional behaviors. Some individuals are euphoric while in dysregulated states. Dysregulation typically is very painful and persons seek to re-regulate as a means of managing the emotional pain.

Self-Regulation as Process

Learning to self-regulate is a process. Temper tantrums in toddlers is normative and is a type of dysregulation. Parents and other adults help infants and young children re-regulate when they have tantrums. Children eventually develop internalized capacities for self-regulation in response to sensitive, contingent caregiver characteristic of secure relationships.

Children with insecure attachments have a much harder time with self-regulation because parents and other adults have not consistently provided the soothing, comfort, and structure necessary for internalization of capacities for self-regulation. In addition, these children may not trust adults to help them manage their strong emotions.

Four General Styles of Self-Regulation

When children and persons of whatever age are under stress, they seek to re-regulate which means to get themselves back on an even keel. For the purpose of the NEATS assessment, schemas that activate themselves in response to stress and trauma can be of four general types: prosocial, antisocial, self-destructive, and inappropriate.

Prosocial responses at their core are secure attachment behaviors, where children seek safe havens that will soothe them and help them to re-regulate. How children re-regulate varies with their experience and development. Young children may soothe themselves through thumb-sucking and seeking a soft toy or blanket. They may want to cuddle.

Older children may also seek attachment figures, but want to talk about what happened and to work out strategies for dealing with situations that triggered the dysregulation. Physical exercise, meditation on something pleasant, drawing, and writing out feelings are some of many different strategies that can contribute to prosocial self-regulation.

When schemas are associated with **antisocial, inappropriate, or self-destructive behaviors,** it becomes important to become aware of expectations, assumptions, and behavioral guidelines that children have internalized and to figure out how help children to redirect and manage behaviors, thoughts, and emotions, associated with particular inner working models.

Children raised in environments where violence is normative are at risk to act out their dysregulation anti-social ways such as defiance, aggression toward others, and destruction of property. Children raised in avoidant, repressive environments may react to their dysregulation through self-destructive actions, such as cutting, using chemicals, and over-eating.

Inappropriate behaviors include being unable to sit still or listen to directions. Sexual acting out can be attempts at re-regulation. Children with these responses believe that parents or other adults cannot or will not help them cope with their dysregulation. Questions about quality of attachment are appropriate in these situations.

Some inner working models, formed during times of stress and trauma remain in their original undifferentiated state. They may sit inactivated for years within brain circuits but may re-activate when individuals perceive themselves to be in situations similar to those that led to their formation in the first place.

Children also learn to regulate, dysregulate, and re-regulate their behaviors through observing parents, siblings, peers, and others with whom they identify, including fictional characters in stories, films, video games, and cartoons. Strategies of self-regulation are linked to family traditions, culture, gender, and age.

Sometimes adults respond appropriately to children's dysregulated behaviors and sometimes they do not. For example, when eight year-old Ramon got down on his hands and knees and barked like a dog, his teacher sent him to the intervention room for what she considered disrespectful behaviors. The intervention room is small, with cement block walls and carpeted floor and a bench screwed into the wall. There is one small window in the door. Children stay in the intervention room until they calm down. Ramon curled up in a ball and cried until he fell asleep.

The teacher did the worst possible thing. Ramon was in a state of dysregulation that is how children experience the triggering of traumatic members. . The imitation of a dog was his way of re-regulating himself. Maybe he was imagining that he was powerful in the face of his reliving of a disturbing episode in his life. The behaviors may appear inappropriate, but in the logic of his own experience, the behaviors were most appropriate.

When dysregulating, children should never be left alone. They may have to be placed in a setting where there can't hurt other children and themselves, but someone should be with them until they calm down. Ramon's behavior was not dangerous but disruptive. Ramon had experienced many traumas that no one had helped him with. The teacher had a teacher's aide. She could have asked the aide to take over the class while she got down on her hands and knees with Ramon and attempted to help him to connect with her and the other people in his environment. He probably was in a dissociative state, far away in his own mind from where he was physically. He was deep within a traumatic episode.

Sometimes adult understand when children are in a state of dysregulation. For example, Terrell tore up the waiting room of a child and family therapy agency when he left his therapy session early and his case manager had left to go the washroom. "I was only gone a minute," the case manager explained.

Terrell, alone in the waiting room, thought the case manager had abandoned him. He relived the trauma related to other abandonments and coped through destroying property. Obviously, abandonment is a therapeutic issue for Terrell. If he develops capacities for self-regulation when is fears of abandonment are triggered, he will have to deal directly with his traumas related to abandonment.

Adults uneducated about children's trauma and dysregulation may have responded in a punitive way. The case manager first assured Terrell that she was there for him. Then she helped him put the waiting room back in order. She planned to talk to him and have him role play what he will do the next time he thinks someone has left him. She understands that helping Terrell with these issues will take a long time. Any help he receives will be most effective if his parents can be involved and if teachers and other adults understand that Terrell has issues regulating himself when traumas related to abandonment are triggered.

Helping Children to Self-Regulate

With intervention, children can learn to self-regulate. Typical interventions include sensitive, contingent responses to episodes of dysregulation that include the assurance of safety, permission to dysregulate while ensuring the safety of self, others, and property, and problem solving and empathy once the dysregulated episode is concluded.

As with other executive function issues, children with self-regulation challenges require safe, structured, predictable environments, clear expectations, and praise for any self-regulation capacities that they show. Parents of children with dysregulation issues will benefit from support groups and psychoeducation. If they have issues with dysregulation themselves, they and their families will benefit from therapy and perhaps self-help groups. Parents with chemical dependency and mental health issues may have particular difficulties with self-regulation, which limits their capacities to help their children with the children's self-regulation.

Professionals, such as teachers and social workers also must educate themselves about issues related to self-regulation and dysregulation and provide themselves with the support and practice guidelines they need to be helpful to children. If they find that their personal responses interfere with their effectiveness, then therapy might benefit them.

Summary

Self-regulation is one of the executive skills. Children under the care of social services often have issues with self-regulation. Capacities for self-regulation are both genetic and environmental in origin. Children with histories of abuse and neglect, inadequate care, and untreated trauma or who have parents who do not model self-regulation and help children to achieve it, are at risk to have difficulties with self-regulation. Interventions that are effective in helping children learn to self-regulate must include both the children and the adults, such as parents, teachers, and others who have responsibility for the care of children with self-regulation issues.

Practice Note

When children have issues with self-regulation, it is important to assess parents for their self-regulation capacities. Children develop optimal self-regulation in the natural course of events in parent-child attachment relationship, in response to parental structure and guidelines, and through observing how parents self-regulate. Issues that children have with self-regulation often find their mirror images in how parents regulate when traumas are triggered.

All too often, services are inadequate and parents are unable to be physically and psychologically available to their children. Many children who grow up in these circumstances still manage to live full and satisfying lives, through great effort and perhaps good luck. Someone or several people step in and are there for them.

Optimal child outcomes are reasons to cheer. Less than optimal outcomes are reasons to figure out what requires more attention and what can be done to foster optimal child and family development.

Note: This article is an excerpt from *The NEATS: A Child and Family Assessment* by Jane Gilgun. The book is available on Amazon, iBooks, Barnes & Noble, and other internet books sellers.

References

A science-based framework for early childhood policy: Using evidence to improve outcomes in learning, behavior, and health for vulnerable children. (2007). Cambridge, MA: Center for the Developing Child at Harvard University. http://www.developingchild.harvard.edu/content/downloads/Policy_Framework.pdfRetrieved on September 23, 2008.

Anderson, Peter (2002). Assessment and development of executive function (EF) during childhood. *Child Neuropsychology, 8(2),* 71-82.

Cicchetti, Dante & Blender, Jennifer (2006). A multiple levels-of-analysis perspective on resilience: Implications for the developing brain, neural plasticity, and preventive interventions. *Annals of the New York Academy of Sciences, 1094,* 248-258.

Cicchetti, Dante & John W. Curtis (2007). Multilevel perspectives on pathways to resilient functioning. *Development and Psychopathology, 19,* 627-629.

Davies, Douglas (2004). *Child Development: A practitioner's guide (2nd ed.).* New York: Guilford.

Dawson, Geraldine (2008). Early behavioral intervention, brain plasticity, and the prevention of autism spectrum disorder. *Development and Psychopathology, 20,* 775-803.

Georgieff, Michael K. (2007). Nutrition and the developing brain: Nutrient priorities and measurement. *American Journal of Clinical Nutrition, 85 (2),* 614s-620.

Hinshaw-Fusilier, Sarah, Neil W. Boris, & Charles H. Neanah (1999). Reactive attachment disorder in maltreated twins. *Infant Mental Health Journal, 20(1),* 42-59.

Hohman, Melinda, Rhonda Oliver, and Wendy Wright (2004). Methamphetamine abuse and manufacture: The child welfare response. *Social Work, 49(3),* 373-381.

Koren-Karie, Nina, David Oppenheim, & Rachel Getzler-Yosef (2004). Mothers who were severely abused during childhood and their children talk about emotions: Co-construction of narratives in light of maternal trauma. *Infant Mental Health Journal, 25(4),* 300-317.

LeDoux, J. (2002) *Synaptic self: How our brains become who we are,* New York, Penguin.

LeDoux, J. (1996). *The emotional brain.* New York, Simon and Schuster.

Lieberman, Alicia F. (2004). Traumatic stress and quality of attachment: Reality and internalization in disorders of infant mental health. *Infant Mental Health Journal, 25(4),* 336-351.

Mash, Eric J., & David A. Wolfe (2006). *Abnormal child psychology* (3rd ed.). Belmont, CA: Wadsworth (Thomson Learning)

Massaro, An, Rebecca Rothbaum, & Hany Aly (2006). Fetal brain development: The role of maternal nutrition, exposures and behaviors. *Journal of Pediatric Neurology, 4(1),* 1-6.

Shields, A. and Cicchetti, Dante (1998) Reactive aggression among maltreated children: The contributions of attention and emotion dysregulation, *Journal of Clinical Child Psychology, 27,* 381-395.

Shirilla, Joan J., & Deborah J. Weatherston (Eds.) (2002). *Case studies in children's mental health.* Washington, D.C.: Zero to Three.

Sokol, Robert J., Virginia Delaney-Black, & Beth Nordstrom (2003). Fetal Alcohol Spectrum Disorder. *JAMA, 290(22),* 2996-2999.

Teicher, M. H. (2002) Scars that won't heal: The neurobiology of child abuse: Maltreatment at an early age can have enduring negative effects on a child's brain, *Scientific American, 286*, 68-76.

Internet Resources for More Information

Amen Clinics: http://www.amenclinic.com/ac/
Autism Society of Canada:
http://www.autismsocietycanada.ca/asd_research/asc_initiatives/index_e.ht ml
Center for Early Education and Development, University of Minnesota, Twin Cites, USA. http://cehd.umn.edu/CEED/
Child Trauma Academy.
http://www.childtrauma.org/ctamaterials/Professions.asp
Medline Plus:
http://www.nlm.nih.gov/medlineplus/childmentalhealth.html
National Institute of Mental Health:
http://www.nimh.nih.gov/health/topics/child-and-adolescent-mental-health/index.shtml
Trauma Center at Justice Resource Institute:
http://www.traumacenter.org

2

Family Incest Treatment

Reviewer: "*biased….misinformation staring me in the face….what hope do these men [victimized as children] have.*

Few families participate in family incest treatment because most couples break up when incest is disclosed. When couples want to stay together, family incest treatment can be helpful. The type of family incest treatment that is the subject of this chapter involves several types of coordinated treatment groups and psychoeducation.

The goal is to make living together safe for children and for the parents and children to learn to cope with the fact that the father and husband in the family has sexually abused the children. Perpetrators in family incest treatment programs are fathers and stepfathers. They sometimes can be siblings. During treatment, perpetrators are not allowed to live with their families, and they cannot have unsupervised visits with their children. In some cases, families participate in family incest treatment without perpetrators. Perpetrators may be in prison, or mothers may have divorced their husbands who committed incest.

Perpetrators can only return to their families when the treatment professionals recommend this to courts, and then judges allow perpetrators to return. Perpetrators should never be allowed to live in families with children unless the families have successfully completed family incest treatment.

Sometimes family incest treatment fails. Perpetrators continue to abuse children sexually. In addition, they may be emotionally abusive to their spouses and children. The possibility of such failures requires professionals to ensure that they provide the best programs possible and that they be knowledgeable about risks to abuse again.

A Note of Caution

If survivors or any other family members do not want to participate in family incest treatment, no one should force them. If any family member does not want to be in the presence of a family member who is a perpetrator, their wishes must be respected. Children especially have to be well prepared to participate in treatment that includes perpetrators. Any sign that they are unprepared and could be harmful should immediately halt any plans for contact.

Professionals and non-offending spouses must be vigilant to ensure that children participate by their own free wills, that they are ready to handle being with perpetrators, and that perpetrators do not in any way blame children, shift guilt to them, or sexualize them.

An Overview

Family incest treatment can be helpful when parents want to stay together and the children want relationships with the perpetrators, but want the abuse to stop. It is also helpful for families to participate without perpetrators since many family issues are dealt with in these programs.

This type of treatment is for families where the children have been victimized and the children are still children. Family incest treatment provides opportunities for all family members to participate. Participation in these programs is voluntary for family members, but perpetrators are almost always court-ordered into treatment. Several families participate in treatment programs at the same time.

In family incest treatment programs, there are peer groups for perpetrators, for non-offending spouses, for survivors, and for siblings who were not sexually abused. Couples therapy, individual therapy, family therapy, multiple family therapy, and family life education are other components of family incest treatment programs.

Treatment can be intensive, lasting four or more hours every week. One break for a community-style meal is common. Typically, each group takes place weekly for about ninety minutes. On alternative weeks, there may be multiple family groups and family life education groups. Couple and individual therapy may take place on another day on a regular basis or occasionally.

Multiple family groups are just that—two to three families meet usually every other week to discuss their issues. On alternative weeks, family incest treatment programs provide education about various aspects of living together in families. This is called psychoeducation where professionals provides information about human sexuality, emotional development, managing emotions, dealing with trauma, setting boundaries, sexual development, sexual abuse, and recovery from sexual abuse. Besides professionals, guest speakers, often graduates of the family incest treatment program, are regular features of the psychoeducation.

Two Case Examples

Family therapy and multiple family groups provide opportunities for family members to build understandings and in some cases to begin the process of repairing relationships. Sometimes a single family member participates. Individuals who attend on their own benefit from hearing about the experiences of non-related family members. As one example, a bright, sixteen year-old college-bound teenage survivor named Sarah was the sole member of her family in a family incest treatment program. Her father had sexually abused her, and he was in prison. Her mother and siblings chose not to participate. In a multiple-family group, a father perpetrator who was a member of another family said to Sarah

> I took advantage of my daughter. Your father took advantage of you. It is important for you to understand this so you can go on with your life and have a good life.

This was a transforming moment for Sarah. She felt a tremendous relief, as if a huge weight had been taken from her. She had felt guilty and responsible. To hear these words from a man who had sexually abused his own children was powerful, much more powerful than hearing the same thing from a professional or from anyone else.

In family therapy, parents and children have opportunities to work on repair of relationships. The following is an example of what a mother said to her son whose father had sexually abused him.

> You told me Daddy was touching you sexually. I thought you were imagining it. I was wrong. I'm so sorry.

Many parents may want to say this or something similar, but don't know how. Family therapy provides the setting, education, and structure for such repair to begin.

Goals of Family Incest Treatment

The goals of family incest treatment are both programmatic and individualized. Programmatic goals are general in nature and are meant for each family in treatment. Individualized goals are tailored to the specific issues that participants have. The most obvious goals are for the abuse to stop and for the children to be safe.

Other goals are that the parent or parents are sensitively responsive to the children, which includes on-going availability to discuss any aspects of the sexual abuse when they children want to. Other general or programmatic goals include emotion expression, taking responsibility, understanding the incest dynamics, making amends, understanding human sexuality, and safety plans.

Emotion Expression

Incest shatters families. At first, family members may be so stunned that they are emotionally numb and confused. Gradually, many emotions surface, such as hurt, rage, anger, shame, humiliation, betrayal, remorse, self-blame, and guilt. Family incest treatment helps family members deal with these chaotic emotions through psychoeducation about expectable responses to incest and through the more individualized opportunities that arise in individual, family, multiple-family, and peer group therapy. They also can see that members of other families have similar reactions. They are not alone.

It is especially important that children and other family members express their emotions to perpetrators, that parents express their emotions appropriately and respectfully to their children, and that children express their emotions to their parents and to each other.

Dealing with the emotions connected to incest is not a simple matter. It can take a long time for family members to feel emotional peace. Emotions related to incest may arise unexpectedly at any time. Family members require education about these powerful emotions and strategies for managing them. Especially important is to learn to be honest but not cruel in the expression of emotion.

Eventually, professionals structure the various groups so that family members can express their emotions to each other directly. In this way, successful graduates of family incest treatment have increased capacities for emotional honesty and directness, which is the foundation of healthy relationships.

Responsibility

Responsibility for the abuse is the perpetrators' alone. For perpetrators, reaching this goal means they make clear statements about their responsibility, make no excuses, and do not rationalize, minimize, or project blame or any motivations on other people. An example of blame and projection is Christian's statement that he hated how his wife smelled, and that is one reason why he avoided sex with her and sexually abused his stepson. An example of a statement of responsibility is for Christian to state

> I was selfish and insensitive. I took advantage of my son. He was afraid to say no to me. I hurt him. I am sorry. I will do whatever I have to do to make sure I do not hurt him or any other child again. I abused my power. I knew deep down I had power over him and he would do what I wanted, but I wanted the incredible pleasure I got from sexually abusing him. What he wanted and needed from me did not matter. All that mattered was what I wanted. I fooled myself into believing he enjoyed the sex as much as I did, but in my heart I knew better. He wanted me to love him as a child not through sex. He required my guidance and not exploitation. My wife had nothing to do with my abuse of our son. I am so sorry. I will do whatever it takes not to hurt my son or any other child ever again.

15

Christian did not say this. If he could have, he would have shown that he had taken responsibility for his behaviors. Such a statement shows unqualified acceptance of responsibility and recognition of abuse of power.

Perpetrators who make such statements also have appropriate affect and show a range or feelings. In addition, they do not feel victimized about the consequences they face for the incest, and they take responsibility for any harm they caused, not only to survivors, but to other family members as well. They take responsibility for any family disruptions their behaviors may have caused. Finally, they show that they live up to these words in many different situations with many different people over time. In short, they are kind and considerate, set appropriate boundaries on others, and respect the boundaries and wishes of others.

Non-offending spouses. The goal of taking responsibility is much different for non-offending spouses. For them, taking responsibility means that they realize that they are not responsible for their partner's incestuous behaviors. They also do not believe that they could have stopped the incest if they had been more sexually available or alluring of if they had been better partners in general. They understand that even if they have been psychologically and emotionally unavailable and even emotionally abusive, this does not justify perpetrators' behaviors. This does not take away any of perpetrators' responsibility.

Spouses do take responsibility for any insensitivity they may have shown to their partners and children by admitting that this has happened and apologizing for it. This is not the same thing as taking responsibility for the incest. The statement earlier of the mother who apologized to her son for not believing him at first is an example. Spouses learn to deal with expectations that mothers should be able to protect their children and honestly grapple with the widespread belief that "The mother always knows." The mother does not always know and can be shocked to their cores when they realize that someone they love and trust has sexually abused one or more of their children. Treatment providers have to be emotionally responsive and sensitive to spouses when dealing with spousal responsibility.

If spouses want to maintain a relationship with their partners, they often choose to engage in individual therapy and other activities to help them deal with their own issues so that they have increased capacities for emotional sensitivity, especially in regard to the issues that their children face. With these increased capacities, they can become emotionally available to their children. They do whatever it takes to keep themselves healthy so that they can be a safe haven for their children.

With increased capacities, they also make more reasoned and informed judgments about whether they want to separate permanently from their partners or attempt to re-build their relationships. They have increased capacities for dealing forthrightly with any issues that their spouses present as perpetrators in recovery.

In addition, non-offending spouses do not place responsibility for the incest on anyone else but perpetrators. They demonstrate their convictions that survivors are not to blame for the incest or any family disruption that may result from the incest. They do not in any way rationalize perpetrators' behaviors, such as saying he was abused as a child. They accept that the consequences of abuse can be very difficult and seek resources to help themselves cope during what can be a very difficult time. Finally, they fulfill their family responsibility and participate in social activities and hobbies they enjoy.

Survivors. Survivors' acceptance of responsibility means they understand that they are not responsible for the incest. They understand that others may blame them, but through treatment and psychoeducation they learn how to cope with the pervasive blame that they may face. They know who they can talk to and who are safe havens. They call upon these people when they are feeling as if maybe they are to blame. They also realize that nothing about them caused the incest and that they are worthy human beings who experienced unfair treatment through being sexually abused and often through the reactions of others to the sexual abuse. They are not damaged goods, but hurt children on the road to healing. They learn to respect and love themselves again.

Survivors do not believe that they are responsible for family break-up if this occurs, nor for any consequences that perpetrators or their families may experience as a result of the incest. Finally, survivors participate in activities that they enjoy, establish or maintain peer relationships, and do well in school.

Siblings. Siblings who were not sexually abused do not blame survivors, mothers, or themselves in any way. In particular, they do not blame survivors for any family disruption and when perpetrators are arrested, jailed, appear in court, and are sentenced. Nor do they blame survivors if they saw perpetrators "playing favorites" while the incest was going on and they were unaware of the incest.

Siblings do not believe that if they had been better children the abuse would not have happened. They do not justify or rationalize perpetrators' behaviors. They understand and accept the consequences that perpetrators face. They are sensitively responsive to survivors. Finally, siblings participate in activities that they enjoy, establish or maintain peer relationships, and do well in school.

Other family members. Other family members, such as grandparents, aunts, and uncles have similar goals, although they typically do not participate in treatment. Perpetrators and non-offending spouses can take the lead in helping their extended families and families of origin understand who is responsible for incest and clear up blame and misunderstandings. Incest treatment programs often have one or more sessions for extended family members in order to develop understanding and to repair relationships.

Understanding the Incest

Another programmatic goal is that family members show an understanding of the incest that occurred in their families. Perpetrators show an understanding of the incest by how they describe their own behaviors and thinking and how they describe the behaviors and thinking of others. In particular, they can describe how they violated family boundaries, abused their power, and took advantage of children. They also understand intergenerational transmission and how their own families of origin may have been the training ground for the subsequent incestuous behaviors.

These understandings are not excuses, but statements of facts on which to build self-understandings and, more practically, safety plans; that is, plans for never again sexually abusing children. Much of the groundwork that led to their abusive behaviors may have occurred outside of their awareness. Their job is to become aware of why they abused children sexually and learn how to manage them. They are responsible for their behaviors no matter where they believe the behaviors originated. No matter how much they enjoyed the incest and no matter how much sexual abuse made them feel better, they can never again be sexual with children.

Non-offending spouses. Non-offending spouses as parents benefit from education about how other parents respond to the incest and about couple and family dynamics before the incest came to light. They also learn this through multiple family groups. They see that they are not alone and have a realistic understanding of what was going on in their own families while the incest was occurring. The more they understand the incest that occurred in their families, the more likely they are to be emotionally available and responsive. Spouses as parents require education about what incest means to children, both survivors and siblings, and then they learn to discuss these issues for their individualized meanings to their children.

Non-offending spouses understand how their partners learned to be abusive and learn not to excuse the behaviors. They deepen their sense of who their partners are and what they can tolerate or not from their partners. Understanding the basis of the incest can help spouses make clear-headed decisions about what is next for them in terms of whether they want to maintain a relationship with their partners. If they choose to do so, they understand the incest so that they can serve as safe havens for their partners when their partners need to put their safety plans to work. Spouses should not underestimate how hard this is.

Survivors and siblings. For survivors and children, understanding the incest that occurred in their families helps them put their experiences into perspectives that they have not had before. They understand that perpetrators have abused their power, violated generational boundaries, and took advantage of survivors. Through psychoeducation, they know what family boundaries and structures are and how to respect them as well as to know when someone violates them. They have their own safety plans and understand how boundary violations may be a sign that they are no longer safe.

They understand any family history related to incest. They do not use any of their knowledge about family history to justify incest in any way, but as part of their self-understanding and as important information about themselves with which they must deal honestly if they are to protect themselves from sexual abuse and any other boundary violations in the future. They know what to do if they think they might be at risk to sexually abuse. They seek out trusted others and do whatever it takes not to repeat the intergenerational cycle of abuse.

Making Amends

The prime persons to make amends are perpetrators. Making amends is a process that takes place in peer groups, family therapy, and multiple family groups over many sessions and is carried into everyday interactions and family life. Making amends builds on statements of responsibility. Other family members may have acted in ways that hurt others, and they, too, when the timing is right, grapple with these issues and figure out how to build bridges and repair relationship.

Once family members are clear about the amends they want to make, they then make them, usually at first within the safety and structure of family or couples therapy. They rehearse their amends making in peer group. They then live their everyday lives in ways that show that they have accepted responsibility and have not reverted to the old and hurtful ways of behaving.

Understanding Human Sexuality

When sexual abuse occurs, children and parents obviously are aware of what abusive sexuality is. Family incest treatment programs not only help participants deal with the hurt surrounding the sexual aspects of the abuse, but they also provide information about healthy sexuality. On the individual level, whatever hurt that participants may have experienced regarding their sexuality is potentially a topic for therapy.

This can involve issues regarding whether survivors are damaged goods, any fears they may have about their sexual attractiveness and future sexual activity, and concerns about whether they are gay, lesbian, or bisexual. Survivors and siblings also may have diminished desire to even want to love and trust others.

If spouses decide to stay with their partners, the incest has damaged their sexual relationship. This must be dealt with for the health of their relationship and their relationship with the children. Non-offending spouses also may have concerns about their sexual attractiveness and capacities for love and trust. Perpetrators may have guilt about their sexual betrayals.

Issues related to sexuality are dealt with individual, family, and peer group both as therapeutic and educational issues. Couples therapy is required for couples to re-build or build sexual intimacy as well as emotional intimacy and communications skills. During the first several sessions, non-offending spouses may express a great deal of hurt and anger.

Perpetrators must be prepared to deal with these recriminations. They did do something terrible. The rage and hurt of partners is a natural occurrence that will gradually diminish in intensity. Perpetrators who have hope that they can remain with their partners in their families will express a great deal of shame, guilt, and remorse that also will diminish over time. Eventually, the couple will get down to what's next—how are they going to rebuild their relationship.

Safety Plans

In family incest treatment, each family member typically has a safety plan. This is of obvious importance to perpetrators. Safety plans are composed of signs that a situation is not safe and what to do when safety is at risk. Safety plans are individualized because each person may have his or her own indicators of potentially harmful situations.

Perpetrators. A typical sign for perpetrators that they are at risk to act out is sexual preoccupation that includes sexualizing children and preoccupation with sexual thoughts. High stress situations can trigger the risk to perpetrate for some. Perpetrators in recovery have clear plans for what to do, such as to call someone they trust and talk about their preoccupation and what brought it on. Perpetrators may talk to spouses about any sexual thoughts and feelings that they may be having. Spouses are an important part of safety plans for recovery perpetrators who have partners.

There is a great deal of professional experience and some research that backs up the effectiveness of confiding in others when individuals are about to do something harmful and stupid.

Spouses. For non-offending spouses, their responsibility is to keep themselves and their children safe. If they notice anything that concerns them about the perpetrators' behaviors, they speak up and deal directly with it. If perpetrators respond poorly, then they follow the next step of the plan. For example, they may contact someone they trust to discuss their options, they may have to leave the family home or ask their partners to leave, or ask the perpetrator to get in contact with a confidant, such as a partner or another perpetrator in recovery.

Survivors and siblings. Survivor and sibling plans involve keeping themselves safe. When they feel unsafe, they talk things over with people they trust. They may tell their parents they don't feel safe and why. If parents respond poorly, they may contact professionals they trust and ask for help. Sometimes they can stay with another trusted family member or neighbor if they do not feel safe in their own homes.

Other family members. Other family members also have a responsibility to keep children safe. It is important that they talk to the parents if they have any concerns about children's safety. If the parents do not respond, their next step is to contact child protection agencies. Family members can also work out cooperative arrangements with parents, such as including survivors and their siblings in their own family events. In some cases, when parents of families where incest have occurred have concerns about children's safety, they may be willing to provide a home for the children.

Summary

In summary, incest is a complicated, difficult family issue. When families want to stay together and repair family relationships, the first line of response is family incest treatment. The overall goal is safety and many issues have to be addressed to ensure safety. Sometimes not all family members participate, and children and adults must freely choose to participate. The advantages of family incest treatment are multiple, including learning from other families that they are not alone and that there is hope for a fulfilling future.

Family incest treatment requires highly competent professionals. It is a disaster and a tragedy that incest reoccurs after a family has participated in incest treatment. Therefore professionals must notice and follow up on any hint that something is off in family relationships. Until they are convinced that it is safe for perpetrators to return to their families, they must not recommend to judges for family reunification.

3

How to Raise a Sex Offender
It's Easy. Prevention is hard

Reviewer: *"not actually all that bad....naïve...lack of understanding of human behavior"*

Note: This article begins as satire and then becomes straightforward.

It's easy to teach children to become sex offenders. First, teach them that using others for their own gain in the way to go. What matters is what they want. What others want does not matter.

Second, avoid talking about sex with your children or make sure you have loads of sexual material and sexual activity in your family home. Talk about loose women, easy sex, and how much sex you have. This really encourages children to think about sex. Combine that with knowing they are supposed to take what they want, they are on their way to becoming sex offenders.

Three, make sure you teach your children not to talk about things that bother them. Shame them if necessary. Tell them in many different ways how proud you are of them that they've got guts because they don't show emotions like fear, sadness, or shame. Sometimes you don't have to say a thing. Just act that way yourself. Your kids will pick up on how to behave.

Four, be too busy with your own affairs to find out what they are doing, what interests them, and what bothers them. Better yet, yell at them, hit them, ignore them, and call them names. You could do one or more of these things. It doesn't really matter. The important thing is to make sure they feel unimportant, like a little black dot that no one notices. This contradicts number 1, I know, but sex offenders are full of contradictions. That's part of what encourages them to be sex offenders.

Five, if your children have experienced traumas, such the death of a parent, repeated changes of caregivers, child sexual abuse, and witnessing violence, be sure to say the child needs to put all of this in the past. Talking about these things just makes them worse. And stick to it. Avoid professional help at all costs.

Six, if you have been sexually abused, had many separations and losses as a child, or other events like that in childhood, make sure you never deal with them. Do not get professional help. This only makes things worse. By doing this, you will be sure to be so busy thinking about your own problems that you will not pay attention to your children. Or, you will be convinced that you went through a lot as a kid, so what's the big deal that my kids have had some sad things happen.

If you want to be extra sure that your children become sex offenders, here are a few other things you can do.

Seven, make sure your children do not want to disappoint you. You can do this by telling them they should never do anything wrong and when they do be disappointed. Then punish them. Not talking to them for a few days is especially effective. If something bad happens to them, you can be sure they will not tell you because then they will be afraid.

Eight, show your children in many ways how fragile you are or how dangerous, preferably both. If something bad happens to your children, they will not tell you because they do not want to hurt you any further than you already have been hurt, or they will not tell you because they do not want you to hurt them or other people. Either way—be fragile or dangerous in your children's eyes, and they will not tell you anything.

Nine, if other people blame your children for something, make sure that other people know that everyone else is at fault, but not your children and certainly not you. Make sure your children never learn to be accountable. Above all, make sure you show them that accountability is for cowards. Never, never apologize. Apologies are for weaklings.

Ten, protect your own image at any costs. If other people say your children have done something wrong, accuse them of bias—any kind of bias. Racial, religious, gender, and income level are great ways to disable anyone who criticizes you.

Just follow these steps. They practically guarantee that your child will be a sex offender, unless your children have the misfortune to find other people who will coddle them and actually encourage them to go against all that you have taught them. Keep your children away from kind, loving people. Believe me when I tell you this. These people will promote their own agendas and persuade your children to talk about things that bother them and will help your children to realize that negotiating for what they want is rewarding, and they can't have everything they want when they want it. You don't want your kids to grow up weak, emotional, and imperfect.

If your children don't turn out to be sex offenders, don't worry—they will become real pains in the neck to a lot of other people, and they may even beat people up or commit financial crimes that bring down a nation or the world. They could even star one day on America's most wanted. In prison, they could be Bubba's bitch or, even better, Bubba himself. They could be head of Toastmasters at a federal prison. Your children have a lot to look forward to.

If social policy helps you raise sex offenders, all the better. Mike's story is an example of what you can hope for. Mike came from a small town where his family had lived for generations. His parents did all they could to ensure that he become a sex offender. They followed all of the above steps. They even had help from the school principal. Mike, a third grader, told the principal that his mother beats him. The principal did not believe Mike. He had known Mike's mother all his life. He even went to the senior prom with her in high school. He knew the mother would never beat Mike. He phoned Mike's mother to tell her what Mike had said.

When Mike got home, his mother beat him for talking to the principal. Mike never again looked to other people to help him. Instead, he made himself feel better by spying on his older brothers having sex with girlfriends. He masturbated to the soft porn that was in the home. Masturbation made him feel better, too. At 13, he was in juvenile detention for sexually assaulting a 12 year-old girl. At 19, he began serving a 15-year sentence for rape.

These steps work. The next section has suggestions about how not to raise sex offenders.

How Not to Raise Sex Offenders
If we keep on the current course,
we will continue to produce sex offenders

Prevention of sexually abusive behaviors is in the forefront of public discussions today. The costs of committing sex offenders to indefinite detention is draining public budgets and taking funds away from education and public safety. For the public good, resources must shift to prevention and not remain focused on detention. If we continue on the current course, we will keep on producing sex offenders.

Prevention includes preventing the development of sexually abusive behaviors in the first place. Sexual abusers were children once. They are not born as sexual abusers. They learn to abuse children sexually. This learning begins in childhood. They learn that sexual behaviors with children feel good, lift their mood, or make them feel loved. They learn to be self-centered and self-absorbed. They do not care what the children want. They learn to be emotionally detached from others. They learn the beliefs that lead them to abuse children.

Most U.S.-based child sexual abuse prevention programs teach children how to avoid being sexually abused. As important as children's self-protection is, this places far too much responsibility on children, allows adults not to take responsibility for protecting children, and ignores those who truly are responsible: perpetrators. The focus of prevention must be on the prevention of sexually abusive behaviors in the first place. Child sexual abuse is preventable. Adults have the responsibility for prevention.

Emotional Expressiveness

The chief factor that appears to protect children from becoming perpetrators of child sexual abuse is emotional expressiveness. When children, adolescents, and adults have capacities for emotional expressiveness, this means they

- have experienced sensitive, responsive, and contingently reciprocal relationships with other people over time, typically with their parents and also with others; This shows a history of secure attachments;

- can experience, identify, and express appropriately a range of feelings;

- understand and identify with (empathize with) the emotions of others;

- encourage the healthy emotional expression of others;

- develop beliefs that happiness involves being sensitive and responsive to others and abhorrence of hurting others; building bridges and being accountable when actions or words cause hurt;

- develop expectations that other people are sensitive and responsive; when others are insensitive and non-responsive, to be capable of standing up to them and calling them out; and

- have good executive skills as shown by their flexible thinking and problem-solving abilities that includes capacities for considering alternative and for thinking through consequences of their actions.

When individuals have capacities for emotional expressiveness, histories of secure attachments, and good executive skills, they realize that acting without considering the effects on others may hurt others and is unfair. When they are stressed, anxious, and angry, they engage their executive skills and seek pro-social ways of coping, such as talking to

25

others, considering alternative actions and the consequences of these actions, and any number of other strategies.

They do not use children to "fix" how they feel, as do many perpetrators of child sexual abuse. In short, they re-regulate in pro-social ways. They resist pro-violence influences to which they have been exposed because they have the emotional resources and executive skills to do so.

Some perpetrators do not abuse children as a means to re-regulate. These abusers abuse simply because abuse makes them feel good. Such abusers have obvious deficits in their emotional development and executive skills. They are unable to understand and empathize with the emotions and rights of others. They do not have the executive skills to see the harm they inflict when they use children sexually. What they want over-rides any consideration of effects on children. They absorb pro-violence beliefs because they do not have the emotional resources and executive skills necessary to see how harmful these beliefs are.

Many perpetrators provide vivid portraits of their parents as emotionally insensitive and non-responsive. Other perpetrators may have had "good enough" parents, but they still abuse children. Some perpetrators, however, are unable to provide researchers and practitioners with the fine details of the relationships with parents and others. Some paint broad brush strokes in terms of their parents' and siblings' adequacy, such as spending time with them and going to church with them, and they do not tell any stories that showed they abused or neglected them or were otherwise insensitive and non-responsive.

What may happen in these cases is that parents have been permissive, and not authoritative. Authoritative parents combine unconditional love, clear rules, simple rewards for following rules, and appropriate penalties for breaking rules.

Since some perpetrators are unable to provide the details needed to draw direct conclusions and because they show an incredible insensitivity and lack of responsiveness themselves, the logical conclusion is that they did not experience their parents as sensitive and responsive and did not as a result develop these capacities themselves. This does not mean that their parents had no capacities for emotional responsiveness. It does mean that some perpetrators as children were unable to respond to whatever parents and others were able to offer them that might have helped them to develop emotionally and to develop good executive skills.

Gender

In general, boys are at a disadvantage as compared to girls in their opportunities for optimal emotional development and for the acquisition of good executive skills in interpersonal relationships. Gender has a role to play in understanding and preventing child sexual abuse. Boys and men perpetrate up to 90% of all sexual abuse. Boys and men are taught to be strong and to be forthright and even aggressive about pursuing what they want. They are socialized to be silent and even ashamed of emotions that might suggest vulnerability. They learn that others may call them "sissies," "girls," "fems," "punks," and "gays" if they show sadness, shame, hurt feelings, need for comfort, and fear.

Dogs and horses are like that, too. They hide their vulnerabilities because vulnerabilities endanger the pack or the herd by attracting predators. Hiding vulnerability may be related to a "warrior" mentality, where men have to be strong at all times to fulfill their roles as conquerors, protectors, and procurers of bounty. If they fail in these roles, they risk swift and harsh consequences.

Because of gender-based socialization, boys are less likely than girls to seek others out to work through their fears, worries, and vulnerabilities. Over time, they become inept at handling these emotions constructively and also risk not to develop their executive skills to think through how to cope with, adapt to, and overcome strong emotions. Some distance themselves from their emotions and may even cease to feel them.

As a result, they find it difficult if not impossible to identify with and be compassionate toward the emotions of others and to be concerned with how their sexual abuse affects children. Many perpetrators show this profound emotional insensitivity and lack of imagination associated with stunted executive skills.

Beliefs

Beliefs have a great deal to do with becoming perpetrators of child sexual abuse. These beliefs lead some individuals to over-value their own interests and discount the worth, wishes, rights, and autonomy of others. Beliefs that lead to child sexual abuse develop in children in many ways. Some children learn them through seeing how their parents behave and listening to what they say. They may witness sexual and physical violence and other actions that discount others. The media help develop beliefs of entitlement. Advertisements, comic books, television shows, toys, the Internet, and video and computer games routinely show sexual exploitation, and sexual and physical violence. Men of action perpetrate violence against "weaker" men and women. These media glamorize violence and show its rewards. Many children come to believe that various types of violence offer survival, status, material rewards, and self-enhancement.

Children who grow up in safe, sensitive, and responsive families and communities are exposed to these influences, as are children who grow up in families and communities where violence is routine and an everyday occurrence. Children who have secure attachments have opportunities to process the violent and other discounting behaviors they witness. They learn from direct instruction not to hurt others. Parents and others model and teach appropriate ways of expressing themselves and getting what they want. Their parents and others are there for them to show them that violence hurts other people. Such children are at relatively low risk to internalize the pro-violence beliefs and actions to which they are exposed.

The lessons of violence do not become part of their inner working models of themselves, others, and how the world works. These individuals grow into adults who say "The thought never crossed my mind" when asked why they have never sexually abused children. They say the same thing when asked about rape. Some may admit that they sometimes say such words as, "I am so angry I could kill him or her." They sometimes have violent thoughts and emotions. They do not act on these thoughts and emotions because they have automatic protective responses that help them to realize that such actions hurt others and themselves.

However, if children's inner landscape matches the outer landscape of the violence and discounting to which they are exposed, children are more likely to believe that violence and discounting are not only permissible but obligatory if they are to have self respect and are to protect themselves. Since violence is heavily gendered, boys are more likely to identify with aggressors and believe they should be aggressive themselves. Entitlement to take what they want becomes part of their inner working models. If they discover that sex with children feels good to them, they take what they want.

Some perpetrators experience themselves as sad and lonely and not powerful. They say that the only time they feel good is when they are sexual with children. Whether abusers are sad and lonely or believe themselves to be big and strong, they still have beliefs that they can take what they want and they have callous disregard for children. They learned to have callous disregard. Parents may not intend their children to be this way, but somehow, possibly through the several steps outlined at the beginning of this article, their children learned to become selfish and entitled to sexually abuse.

Prevention

Everyone has a part to play in prevention. Our social system is complex. Our responses, therefore, have to be on many different levels that reflect not only the complexity of our social organization but also the complexity of the influences that lead to the sexual abuse of children. Prevention of child sexual abuse requires actions on the individual, familial, community, statewide, countrywide, and international levels. Anything individuals or groups do to promote children's well-being contributes to prevention. Something as small as a kind word to a child or as long-term as advocating for policy and program changes contribute to prevention.

Universal Prevention

The information in this article provides a foundation for many different kinds of social actions that can contribute to the prevention of the sexual abuse of children. Some policies and programs are already providing such services, often, however, without realizing how important the programs are to child sexual abuse prevention. To be more mindful that emotional expressiveness, healthy sex educations, executive skills, and awareness of how respect and empathy contribute to child sexual abuse prevention can make these programs more effective and responsive. Such programs are example of universal or primary preventions strategies, or strategies that are aimed at the general population. Unfortunately, such programs do not exist in sufficient numbers to meet the need.

Selective Prevention

Selective prevention efforts target at-risk individuals, meaning individuals whose life circumstances and beliefs could lead to adverse outcomes or already have. *Secondary* and *tertiary prevention* are terms used to describe types of selective prevention. Secondary prevention involves policies and programs designed to promote optimal development in individuals at risk for poor outcomes. Tertiary prevention involves policies and programs for persons how already have poor outcomes.

Examples of secondary prevention are parent education groups and other psychoeducation programs where individuals receive information and skills training that help them to cope with, adapt to, and overcome the effects of their own experiences of abuse and neglect. When parents and others participate successfully in these programs, they become more emotionally expressive and less-self-absorbed and therefore more sensitively responsive to their own children, to their life partners, and to other people in general. They also learn strategies for dealing with the many challenges involved in raising children.

Tertiary prevention involves interventions for individuals, children, teens, adults and their families, where a condition has already appeared, such as sexually abusive behaviors. Examples are treatment programs for children and their families where the children have been sexually abused or who experienced other adversities. These programs are described in some detail in chapter twelve. Incapacitation involves removing individuals from society and keeping them confined. Prison and civil commitment are examples of tertiary prevention that involves incapacitation.

Individualization

While there are themes that cross over into different types of prevention efforts, individualization is another principle associated with successful secondary and tertiary prevention programs. One size does not fit all. When crafting and implementing programs and interventions, professionals who are flexible and who tailor what they offer have good chances for success.

Typically, effective treatment programs explore clients' capacities for emotional expressiveness, sensitivity to others, executive skills, beliefs about entitlements and taking what you want, and capacities to deal constructively with stress and trauma. In other words, they explore gender-based beliefs, such as men as heads of households who have absolute control over wives and children. Dealing with selfishness and self-centeredness is part of effective treatment programs.

Effective treatment professionals, however, are open-minded enough not to make assumptions about the families of perpetrators, nor about the experiences and beliefs that perpetrators have that might contribute to their sexually abusive behaviors. Professionals must do individualized assessments and be prepared to devise strategies meant to increase the capacities that research and professional experience have identified as factors in the sexual abuse of children. Sensitive responsiveness is the centerpiece of treatment goals, but how professionals nurture sensitive responsiveness in clients requires sensitive responsiveness on their part.

Society's Executive Skills

As a society, we lack good executive skills. We do not see how accepted beliefs and practices result in the sexual abuse of children. Parents and professionals alone cannot change the forces that lead to sexual abuse, although they do what they can to counter these forces within their immediate spheres of influence. Society-wide efforts are required for prevention.

Several issues must be handled well to ensure that children do not sexually abuse others. This includes the sex education of children, encouraging the emotional expression of boys, and challenging beliefs and practices that lead to the sexual abuse of children. The mass media, government, higher education, and religious institutions can make major contributions to child sexual abuse prevention.

The Four Cornerstones of Prevention

Healthy sex education is one of four cornerstones of child sexual abuse prevention. Most parents require a great deal of encouragement and education to talk to their children about sexuality and sexual abuse. Local, national, and international governments, foundations, school boards, religious institutions, and advocacy groups could develop public awareness campaigns to promote healthy sex education in families and in schools and to make educational materials widely available. Through the internet, these groups could make videos, podcasts, and other materials available to anyone who wants them.

Sex education is still controversial for some, but it is time to pay attention to research and experience that shows that healthy sex education promotes healthy sexual behaviors and reduces unwanted consequences of irresponsible and uninformed sexual behaviors, such as sexual harassment, child sexual abuse, rape, unwanted pregnancies and sex-related diseases.

The second cornerstone is the promotion of emotional expressiveness in boys. Healthy emotional development automatically leads to the acquisitions of good executive skills. This alone would go a long way toward helping children overcome a major risk for abusing others. There could be a massive effort to support sensitive, responsive parenting. Many parents are already, but all parents and their children benefit when there are widely available resources for parents that help them to maintain their sensitive responsiveness.

This is an up-hill battle because of the many sources of distorted depictions of masculinity and femininity, the rewards for meeting gendered expectations, and the punishments for failing to do so. Many gendered expectations interfere with the development of emotional availability and sensitivity.

As discussed earlier, there are many barriers to boys' emotion expressions and many rewards from them to be aggressive and to take what they want. Direct discussion of pro-violence beliefs and alternatives to these beliefs are part of emotion education. Many of the words that punish boys for not conforming to gender expectations, such as "sissies," "fem," and "girls" are sexist; meaning what it means to be male is defined as not being female. Being female is stigmatized. Such gendered strategies of social control are destructive.

A third cornerstone is to devise strategies to encourage and support parents who have experienced trauma to deal with trauma's effects.

31

The other cornerstones—promotion of emotional expressiveness and executive skills and side-spread sex education—could loosen the rigid resistance that many parents have to dealing with their own issues. Traumatized parents were traumatized children once. Those who refuse to deal with their traumas likely received punitive responses when they tried to talk about their traumas.

A fourth cornerstone is parent education programs, which, as mentioned, are already available. They can, however, be promoted more widely and many more can be created. In these programs, parents can learn to become more sensitive and responsive than they might have been otherwise. Well-prepared parents raise children who have capacities associated with the formation of intimate relationships with generational equals and who understand and protect vulnerability in themselves and others.

Parents, professionals, and socially aware citizens have important roles to play in promoting universal and selective prevention programs. They can join task forces and citizen groups, work for candidates who understand what children and families need to thrive, research social issues, and lobby local, statewide, national, and international governments. Blogs, letters to editors, and posting advocacy pieces on the Internet are possibilities. Volunteer work at schools, childcare centers, and social service agencies are other ways of contributing to healthy children, families, and societies. We have complex social systems. Effective change will happen when multiple parts of systems change.

Social Skills

Social skills training is a prevention strategy that many adults can implement. Social skills training can help children develop empathy and executive skills. Parents, educators, and others who spend time with children can adapt these approaches to a variety of situations in families, classrooms, and other settings. They can be used as universal prevention strategies or selective.

Children learn social skills through direct instruction and through observing how others behave. They repeat the behaviors that bring them rewards and behaviors that they see are rewarded. The following are examples of guidelines for teaching children social skills. Parents and teachers may want to provide additional guidelines.

Expectations

Children need to know what parents and teachers expect from them. It is important for parents and teachers to set ground rules. Keep them simple. Here are some examples.

Family Etiquette

- No hitting, yelling, pushing, or biting. If someone bothers you, tell him or her to stop.

- If other children continue to bothers you, tell me. It's my job to take care of things like that.

- If you bother another child, you will have a time out.

- Give other people a chance to finish talking before you talk.

- Do not use other people's stuff without their permission.

- If you have questions about differences between boys and girls, ask me. Do not inspect the bodies of others, especially of children younger than you.

Classroom Etiquette

- Raise your hand if you want to talk in the classroom.

- Do not interrupt when other children are talking.

- Do not interrupt when I am speaking.

- Stay in your seats until I give you permission to get up.

- Do not push, grab, or shove other children.

- If someone bothers you, tell him or her to stop.

- If someone bothers you and will not stop when you tell them to, tell me. I will take care of it.

- If you bother another child, you will have a time out.

When children follow the rules, recognize them for it. Here are some examples.

- "Thank you, Marcus, for raising your hand when you wanted to speak."

- "Good job, Kylie. Ronald pulled your hair. You told him to stop and that it hurt. He didn't stop. You told me."

- "I can see you really wanted to say something, Jamal. Good for you that you waited until Jordan finished what she had to say."

- "I'm glad you asked. I'm happy to talk to you about kissing boys."

In short, when children perform well in classrooms and at home, it is important to praise them immediately. Rewards increase the chances that children will repeat the behaviors.

Direct Instruction

Something as brief as 10-minute sessions of direct instruction once a week or as needed could have life-long benefits for children. Instruction can create a safe and enjoyable classroom experience and family life. The following are some topics to consider.

- How to ask someone for something.

- How to say "no" to someone who asks you for something.

- How to accept a "no" from someone else.

- How to thank someone who does something nice for you.

- How to disagree with someone.

- How to think about consequences of your actions: Who will they affect? How will they affect them? How will they affect you?

- How to introduce people to each other.

- How to joke with others without hurting them.

- How to apologize.

- How to admit you did something wrong.

- How to make up for doing something wrong.

- How to accept an apology.

- How to help another child when someone is hurting him or her.

- How to ask someone to stop doing something that hurts or bothers you.

- How to ask someone for help when someone is hurting or bothering you.

- How to listen to a friend who is feeling sad.

To teach these skills, first describe the topic. Then provide a brief description of how to respond. Then role play in front of the children how to respond. Next, have the children role play with each other. Have the children play both roles. Praise them when they role play well. Help them problem-solve how to do better if they have difficulties in the role plays.

Finally, give the children a few minutes to talk about the activity with each other and with whoever provides the instruction. During these discussions, teachers have the opportunity to explore children's expectations about gendered-based behaviors and entitlements. They can broaden the discussion to ask children to describe the kinds of interactions they observe in video games, on the internet, and in movies.

Direct instruction and discussion of these topics contain implicit and explicit messages about emotional expressiveness, boundaries, respect, and empathy. They are counter messages to beliefs about entitlement and taking what you want regardless of what others want.

Teach by Example

How parents and teachers deal with children teaches them a great deal about social skills. When what you do makes them feel good, they are likely to imitate you. When they see that you reward the behaviors you want, children will want those rewards for themselves. Practice good social skills yourself, and the children will learn from you.

In summary, children learn social skills from direct instruction and from observation. Parents and educators are positioned to teach children skills that they will use for the rest of their lives. In the short term, children with good social skills contribute to enjoyable and safe families and classrooms. Social skills training such as those just described can help children develop good executive skills and emotional expressiveness.

Teaching these skills is part of sensitive, responsive parenting and teaching. These skills, in combination with a good sex education, sensitive care of children who have experienced trauma, and countering abuse-supportive beliefs with pro-social beliefs, go a long way toward prevention. Preventing children from becoming sexual abusers is an important goal in prevention programs.

Teaching Moments

In everyday interactions with children, adults have opportunities to promote emotional expressiveness and executive skills. Children can sometimes be rude, impolite, and aggressive toward other children and adults. When this happens, parents and other adults will be most helpful if they have balanced reactions. Over-reacting or dismissing the significance of the behaviors are common, but what counts is for adults to engage their own executive skills and to keep their cool. Such child behaviors are teaching moments.

Adults are helpful when they ask the child to stop the behavior and name the feeling they think the child is experiencing. Often that is enough. Naming a feeling for a child often calms the child because the child feels understood. In calm states of mind, parents and educators can engage their own executive skills and talk with children about how they can handle their emotions more effectively the next time.

Children are eager to have friends and to belong. To do so, they have to learn how to get along with others. Teaching children how to respectfully express what they want and do not want or what they like or do not like can lead children to build healthy relationships. Respect means that children take into consideration what others want, they know how to negotiate so as to find common ground, and they know not to take advantage of others to get what they want.

Remind children of the rules. Gently guide them to time out if you have set time out as the consequence for such behaviors. Keep the time out brief. Even a minute or two can be long enough. The following guidelines can help in difficult situations with children.

Remind children that all feelings are okay, but they do need to think about how they express their feelings. Expressing themselves with rudeness and disrespect, with verbal aggression, verbal abuse, excluding or ignoring, physical aggression, or sexual aggression are not okay. Telling someone to back off or saying, "I don't like how you're behaving," or

"Don't speak to me that way," or "I find your behaviors hurtful" are direct and clear expressions of feelings that do no harm. They are okay.

Attend to the child who has been hurt. Children who are rude and impolite hurt others. Children who have been hurt gain in self-confidence and self-respect when others comfort them and help them to figure out how to stand up for themselves while also not harming others themselves.

Another variation on acting without thinking is when children and adults, for that matter, "go for the jugular;" that is, act without thinking when someone does something they do not like. They immediately become angry and engage "low road" responses that can involve thinking angry thoughts, calling others names, and hitting and kicking. For some, sexual aggression can result, or sexualized self-soothing. Fortunately, children—and adults—typically can restrain themselves, but they also have no idea how to engage their "high road" responses and thus to negotiate with others to find common ground. They therefore silence themselves. This undermines connection and relationships.

For children to be able to handle such situations, they have to see that people around them have effective strategies for doing so. They also require direct instruction. The instruction would include 1) noticing that they are about to act without thinking, 2) consider what they really want, 3) and think about the various ways that they can get what they want and also maintain a healthy connection with others.

Guidelines that can help in such situations include 1) being clear about what they want, 2) telling other people what they want, 3) listening to others in order to understand what they want, and 4) engaging in a search for ways to accommodate each other. Sometimes what we want is unacceptable or not possible. In those situations, children need to develop capacities to accept such possibilities, but they have the right to know the reasons why certain things cannot happen. Children eventually internalize parental guidelines and direct instruction. They become skilled in handing conflict situations. They also know that they can go to their parents and other adults if they need some help.

Alternative Behaviors

Children may sometimes need direct instruction about their behaviors when they do not realize that their behaviors hurt others. It is important that parents make it clear that some behaviors are not allowed. The next step is to teach behaviors that are allowed to replace them. For example, you could say to a child, "When you do that, it hurts other people." Problem-solving is helpful. How else could they tell others what they want? Children often respond well to examples.

Parents and teachers can have a big impact in seemly small events. Janie, five, yelled at Sylvia, also five, "You're a liar" during play time in kindergarten. Sylvia was indeed lying. However, the kindergarten teacher was so concerned about Janie's rudeness that she gave Janie a time out and told her to sit in the corner behind the grand piano. Janie cried and felt ashamed. The teacher missed an opportunity to teach Janie new social skills. She could have told Janie, "Speaking so loudly and calling someone a liar hurts. If you don't agree with Sylvia, you can say, 'I don't agree.' Instead of providing guidance, the teacher's actions provoked shame and hurt in this young child.

Few children at five have the skills and awareness to respond firmly but empathically to someone whose behaviors concern them. After the teacher's reprimand, Janie still did not know how to express concerns about others' behaviors, but the next time she wanted to disagree she would remember her prior punishment. She would then be at risk to yell ever louder, be even more rude, or to say nothing and seethe. She might even feel guilty and at fault for objecting to another's poor behaviors.

Sylvia, of course, needed some attention and instruction as well. The teacher could have acknowledged that Sylvia might have been hurt by Janie's words, and she could have told Sylvia that when you say something that another child does not believe, the child may challenge you. The teacher might not have known whether Sylvia was lying or not, but she could have helped Sylvia understand that other people may disagree with her but they have no right to be rude and aggressive.

Eventually, the teacher could have worked out a way to repair the children's relationship. When both children had settled down, understood what went wrong, and felt safe, the teacher could have encouraged Janie to apologize for her aggression and also state she disagreed with Sylvia. Sylvia could have admitted she did not tell the truth and would do better the next time. She could have accepted Janie's apology.

This kind of guidance takes teacher time and skill but it is important to do. Children sometimes mistake verbal aggression for humor. Something as simple as helping children understand that words hurt may help children realize that they have to stop doing something.

Final Words

Child sexual abuse is a serious social problem that undermines the well-being and life chances of millions of children in the United States and world-wide. Accurate understanding of sexual abuse, sensitive responsiveness to children, and direct instruction about emotion expression, respectful behaviors, and sexuality are steps toward creating a more just and caring society.

Furthermore, social policy and current prevention programs do not recognize the importance of the prevention of the development of sexually abusive behaviors. If we continue on the current course, we will drain public budgets to keep sex offenders locked up while we continue to do little or nothing to produce even more sex offenders.

Child sexual is a complex social problem that few people understand well. Myths and misunderstandings lead many to believe that they do understand. What child and adult survivors, perpetrators, and mothers say about child sexual abuse adds important dimensions to knowledge and provides a basis for policy, prevention, and intervention. Perpetrators take advantage of children. It is that simple. Perpetrators are selfish. It is that simple. Children require sensitive, responsive care. It is that simple.

While cattle instinctively form protective circles around unrelated young to ward off danger, human beings allow child sexual abuse to continue. Our social systems are more complicated than that of cattle, but our executive skills are superior to those of cattle. When it comes to child sexual abuse, however, our executive skills are poor. We have extreme reactions to perpetrators whom we can identify, typically strangers who abuse children. We spent huge sums of money for prisons and civil commitment, while we provide woefully inadequate services for child survivors and their families. Furthermore, we do not have the executive skills to connect the dots that might prevent the development of sexually abusive behaviors in the first place.

The promotion of boys' emotional development, large-scale commitment of resources to promote healthy sex education, challenges to gender role socialization that put boys at risk to perpetrate, parent education and training, and enlightened efforts to help traumatized parents deal with their own trauma are some of the many strategies that will contribute to primary prevention.

Efforts at every level of our society are required. Advocacy through task forces and citizens' groups, policy changes and resources to implement and monitor programs, training programs for professionals based on accurate, multi-faceted information, and many other efforts are some of the many ways to make a difference. Volunteer work with children and their families in homeless shelters and children's homes, guardian ad litem programs, and reading to children in school are some of the many ways that individuals can make a difference in individual children's lives.

The roots of child sexual abuse are wide-spread and are connected to many other social ills. Almost any effort that promotes child and parent well-being contributes to prevention. Parent support programs, for, example, have positive effects that include and go beyond the prevention of child sexual abuse. There simply are not enough of them. Healthy and appropriate sex education, emotion and social skills education in the schools, and programs that challenge pro-violence beliefs are other interventions that contribute to prevention.

Children who have secure attachments to their parents are much more likely to receive healthy sex educations and to be raised by parents who practice gender egalitarianism. It would never occur to them to take advantage of others. If, as young children, they do attempt to do so, their parents immediately correct them and show them how to behave in respectful ways.

While some children receive exemplary care, there are countless millions of children already at risk because of insecure and disorganized attachments and who receive their sex education and guidance for sexual behaviors from peers and the media. Such children have complex risks for various poor outcomes. Some of them perpetrate child sexual abuse. An educated public with good executive skills would take immediate action to provide children and families with the resources they require to thrive. There is much to be done.

Note: This is a chapter from *Child Sexual Abuse: From Harsh Realities to Hope*, available on Kindle, Amazon.com, and other on-line booksellers.

4

It's Time for the Roman Catholic Church
to Show the World What Penitence is

Review: *"an inflammatory book that is poorly written
and poorly researched"*

5 MAY 2011, MINNEAPOLIS, MINNESOTA, USA. Just when I thought
I had seen the worst of it, I read about the imprisonment of Raymond
Lahey, former Roman Catholic bishop of Antigonish, Canada. Yesterday,
Bishop Lahey pled guilty to one charge of child pornography. He
immediately began to serve a year in prison.

Mr. Lahey got off easy. Canadian border officials discovered on his
laptop almost 600 photos of boys in degrading sexual poses, videos, and
stories about boys having sex with each other. His passport showed he had
visited Thailand, Malaysia, and Indonesia, hotspots for men seeking sex
with children. Mr. Lahey denied an interest in boys, but said he was
attracted to older males. Whatever happened to his promise of celibacy?
How about decency? Respect? The life of Jesus he had publicly espoused?

The Roman Catholic Church, like other religious institutions, has
been a force for good for more than two thousands years. Every religious
organization, as far as I know, teaches the faithful to love one another, to
uphold the dignity and worth of other human beings, and to stand for
social justice. Most of the women and men who dedicate themselves to the
religious life have lived exemplary lives and have done untold good.

At the same time, this church has created an institution where
thousands of their priests, consecrated as they are to God, betray the values
that the church stands for. The record is clear on this church's history of
protecting and covering up the terrible deeds of pedophiles and other
priests who exploit parishioners sexually.

Those in charge of the Roman Catholic Church have an
unprecedented opportunity to show the world what penitence is. I would
like the Roman Catholic Church to do an examination of conscience and
then to reform itself. This is what their priests tell the faithful to do. So

must they. To do this, each member of the Roman Catholic clergy and laity has to be skeptical of her or his relationship with God.

An Examination of Conscience

From early childhood on, the Roman Catholic Church teaches its members that we are sinners and we must identify our sins, experience sorrow for the harm we have caused, confess what we have done, be accountable for what we have done, do penance, and then to take measures that ensure that we do not keep on harming others. When church members do this, we have meaningful lives.

The administrators of the Roman Catholic Church must do the same. Priests, bishops, cardinals, and the pope are sinners. It is not just parishioners who sin. Those who are priests must examine their own consciences in regard to the sexual abuse clergy has committed. This examination of conscience would have several parts. Each part would contribute to what could be a fairly complete picture of what has gone wrong to permit the abuse to happen and what goes right when priests and other religious live exemplary lives.

This examination of conscience can begin with seeking to understand the lives of the priests who have committed sexual abuse. These priests would tell their life stories to well-trained interviewers. Each priest would be interviewed many times until they are satisfied that they have told their life stories as honestly as they can. I have done this kind of research with perpetrators and survivors of child sexual abuse for many years.

It is amazing how grateful people are to have someone listen to them as they share the truth of their lives. It does not seem to matter whether the truth is something they are proud of or not. There is something deeply meaningful about the telling. I expect that many of these priests would be grateful for the opportunity, would express deep sorrow, and seek ways to make up for what they have done. The act of participating in the interviews is a way for penitent priests to make up for the harm they have caused. Such interviews would include members of religious orders who are not priests but are brothers as well as lay members of religious orders who have abused others sexually.

An examination of conscience would also involve life histories of priests who have not sexually abused children and who, according to nominations from parishioners, have been exemplary priests. We need these interviews in order to discern what has gone right and what has gone wrong in the lives of men who have publicly declared themselves to be followers of Jesus and desirous of helping others be followers of Jesus.

The women of the church who have dedicated themselves to following Jesus as nuns and members of lay religious orders would also be sources of ideas about the nature of exemplary lives and the conditions that have allowed so many pedophile priests to operate within the Roman Catholic Church.

Some of these religious women may have been sexually abusive to church members. They, like the male priests and brothers, may want to tell their life stories as ways of making up for the harm they have caused. As with priests, most of them have lived exemplary lives. From understanding the conditions under which individuals live exemplary lives can come principles that may guide others to do the same.

An examination of conscience would also involve interviews with priests, including bishops, archbishops, cardinals, and the pope, about their personal experiences with priests who have sexually abused children and other parishioners. This, too, would involve multiple interviews over time. As with the priests who were active sexual abusers, at least some of those who had responsibility for supervising them are likely to want to share their stories, express their sorrow, and seek ways to make up for what they have done or not done.

Furthermore, an examination of conscience would involve interviews with survivors of priest sexual abuse, their families, and parishioners in general. The number of interviews would vary depending upon the depths to which these persons would want to go and how much and what they want to say. Many of these people might have excellent ideas about what went wrong and how the Roman Catholic Church can correct these wrongs.

Another step in an examination of conscience is to interview religious leaders and theologians within the Roman Catholic Church and members of other faiths to gather ideas about what they think may have gone wrong with a church that permitted such wide-spread abuse. These individuals, too, might have some ideas about how the Roman Catholic Church can correct these wrongs and the conditions under which individuals live exemplary lives.

Theologians may have insight into the importance of being skeptical about our relationship with God, the importance of doubting whether we really are following God's will, and the centrality of allowing others to know what is in our hearts so that they can help us not fool ourselves into thinking we are following God's will when we are not. I discuss skepticism about our relationship with God later in this article.

It is hard to anticipate what kinds of issues will surface through these interviews, both in terms of what went wrong and what the remedies might be, or are worth trying. Yet, I can think of no other way for the Roman Catholic Church to make up for these terrible deeds without this wide-spread examination of conscience.

The interviewers would be well trained to listen and to create a sense of safety so that the persons they interview feel safe and respected. The interviewers should also be from a variety of religious faiths and be trained in the best traditions of social science research. This means they continually examine themselves and each other for biases that might distort what interviewees might want to say. There are standard procedures for researchers to ensure that they deal with their biases.

The results of these interviews would be disseminated in every possible way. These ways include press releases, internet publications, scholarly journals, textbooks, religious education including courses on theology, in the confessional, and through preaching from the pulpit. What ought to come through clearly is the recognition of the deep harm sexual abuse has caused so many, sincere sorrow for the harm, and heartfelt requests for forgiveness.

Those harmed may not want to extend forgiveness in the sense of saying "It's all in the past; it's time to move on." Most will say, "I feel sorry that you cloaked yourself in virtue and took advantage of me. I let go of my hurt and guilt. I did nothing wrong. I hope your penitence is sincere. I want nothing to do with you. I want to surround myself with people who love me more than they love their own sexual and emotional gratification."

Reform

Based on what these interviews might show, the Roman Catholic Church would have a wealth of ideas about how to make up for the terrible deeds that some of their priests have perpetrated and that the structures, procedures, and unstated assumptions of the Church have allowed.

I believe that the principles of accountability, penance, contrition, and reform are already present in the minds and hearts of persons of the faithful. I hope that the administrators of the Roman Catholic Church have the foresight to tap into this wisdom.

The values on which the Roman Catholic Church stands are a powerful force for good. The kind of examination of conscience that I suggest would result in a compilation of wisdom that would not only renew the Church but be a world-wide model of accountability.

Skepticism Toward Relationships with God

I believe that those who perpetrate child sexual abuse had no doubt that their sexual acts were good, not only for themselves but for the children and others they abused. Priests who believe sexual abuse is good obviously do not consider that they may be fooling themselves about God's will for them. They do not have the doubts and skepticism that I believe is inseparable from faith.

I have conducted interviews with perpetrators of child sexual abuse for more than 25 years. With some exceptions, these perpetrators experienced these sexual behaviors as good. They experienced what they thought was intimacy, bliss, the greatest feelings of the world, joy, completeness. In their own minds, what they did was not sexual abuse. The following is a sample of what perpetrators say.

Christian, in his early fifties, described the sexual abuse of his 13 year-old stepson, Seth, as a love affair.

> I didn't call it molesting. It was making love to my son....When I was having my relationship with my son it was like a love affair. It really was. It was real.

He continued.

> What I was doing was different. I was making love to my daughter, to my son.

Joe said

> We never had penile intercourse. I don't know why. I had it stuck in my brain that I couldn't have that. That was incest to me.

In addition, some abusers are outraged when they hear about other instances of child sexual abuse. Mike said

> I used to sit there and watch TV or I'd read something in the paper. I'd say, 'Look at this son of a bitch. He ought to get twenty years,' but I was doing the same thing. Mine wasn't that way. See, mine was love. There's a difference, you know.

Roger Vangheluwe, former Roman Catholic Bishop of Bruges, Belgium, experienced child sexual abuse as "a certain kind of intimacy that took place." He elaborated on this statement on live French television during the fifth week on Lent in 2011.

> I have often been involved with children, and I never felt the slightest attraction. It was a certain kind of intimacy that took place.

I don't have the impression at all that I am a pedophile. It was really just a small relationship. I did not have the feeling that my nephew was against it—quite the contrary.

How did it begin? As with all families, when they came to visit, the nephews slept with me. It began as a game with the boys. It was never a question of rape. There was never any physical violence used. He never saw me naked, and there was no penetration.

I believe that the bishop is speaking the truth as he experienced it. He did not believe that what he did was anything other than intimacy and that he did not harm his nephew.

Some might argue that the men who perpetrate child sexual abuse are misguided. That they are, but what about the priests who had dedicated themselves to God? What about the bishop of Bruges? The bishop in Canada? These men had dedicated their lives to God. The bishops had been consecrated as bishops.

Priests are supposed to examine their consciences and consult with a spiritual advisor or a confessor to make sure they are was fulfilling their promise of living holy lives. They promised to be celibate, meaning no sex with anyone. I believe that priests who committed sexual abuse mistook evil for good. There has to be some mechanism within the Roman Catholic Church that permits this mistaking of evil for good. Many priests have done exactly what the Bishop of Bruges and the Canadian bishop have done. They must believe that their evil acts are good.

There has to be a mechanism or set of assumptions in the Roman Catholic Church that permits some priests to believe that they are consecrated to God and therefore can not do wrong. Certainly, most priests do not believe they can do no wrong. Most priests believe themselves to be sinners along with the rest of us.

A few do not believe they are sinners. Some are likely to believe that the sexual abuse they perpetrate is a form of God's love. Survivors have said that priests who abused them have said this.

Such priests are not skeptical enough of their relationship with God. Human beings see through the glass darkly. It is difficult to discern God's will for us. We have to be full of doubt about God's will and consult openly and honestly with others when we are about to undertake an action, especially an action that involves others.

Imagine how differently today's Roman Catholic Church would be if every priest who has committed sexual abuse first consulted with a spiritual advisor. Imagine if these priests had openly and honestly said they believe that what they want to do is a manifestation of God's love. I believe their spiritual advisors would have guided them to think more deeply and widely about the actions they wanted to take.

Somehow, these priests who committed child sexual abuse had so much pride in their special relationship with God that they did not question themselves when they thought about and then acted out sexually with children and other parishioners. I wonder if they believed they had a right to fulfill their sexual fantasies.

I believe that they believed they were acting out God's love. Maybe not all of them, but a lot of them did. Some of them may have realized they have harmed children and other parishioners.

One More Thing

If the Roman Catholic priestly hierarchy do not believe that examinations of conscience as I suggest, reform, and skepticism about God's will compose a plan they would like to follow, then I suggest internet surveys that anyone who is internet savvy can do. The following are some questions for the survey.

1. how many of survivors of clergy abuse received an apology from the priests who abused them?

2. if they did receive apologies, did these survivors experience these priests as understanding the harm they had caused?

3. if survivors felt as if anybody in the Roman Catholic Church cared about the abuse they experienced;

4. if they ever felt it was safe to talk to anyone about sexual contact or attempted sexual contact with clergy and other religious;

5. if they are afraid to talk to anyone in the Roman Catholic Church out of fear of being blamed for their own abuse;

6. if they believe the abuse is their fault;

7. if they feel dirty because of the abuse;

8. if the Roman Catholic Church ever offered them opportunities to share their experiences with clergy abuse for the purpose of helping the church to understand the nature of abuse.

These are sample questions that would be important to ask. Survivors would benefit from opportunities to share their experiences this way. The church would have data on which to base on-going reform.

Discussion

Examinations of conscience, reform, and skepticism are the kinds of steps the Roman Catholic Church could take in order to make up for the terrible deeds that some members of their clergy have committed. The Roman Catholic Church must do an examination of conscience. The Roman Catholic Church must reform itself based upon what it learns from this examination of conscience. All human beings, including priests, must be skeptical of any special relationship they think they have with God.

Not only would such actions help heal uncounted hundreds of thousands of hurt parishioners throughout the world, but such actions would also be a model of how to do atone for terrible deeds and to make things right.

If the Roman Catholic Church does not want to take these steps, then anyone can post a survey on the internet and start gathering much-needed information.

Final Note

A May 4, 2011 statement from Anthony Mancini, Archbishop of Halifax and Apostolic Administrator of the Diocese of Yarmouth, assured his audience that Raymond Lahey, the former bishop, will be dealt with by the church. He also asked people not to want revenge but forgiveness. The Archbishop did not address the deep wounds and harm that Raymond Lahey had caused. This is one more example of the need for an examination of conscience in the Roman Catholic Church.

Sexual abuse results in soul wounds that affect the quality of life and life chances of survivors. It is time for the administrators of the Church to acknowledge this and to take all means possible to ensure it does not happen to one more person, child, teenager or adult. Such steps involve a humble, thorough examination of the forces that led to such massive hurt to so many within an institution that is supposed to do good. The world is in need of a model of repentance and reform. The Roman Catholic Church is positioned to offer such a gift.

References

Blanchfield, Mike (2011). Roman Catholic bishop Raymond Lahey pleads guilty to child-porn charge. The Canadian Press, May 5. http://www.google.com/hostednews/canadianpress/article/ALeqM5hxA G5f25LDTWM3w0wFVG2DBi7eRQ?docId=6750634

Castle, Stephanie & Rachel Donadio (2011). Bishop in sexual abuse case prompts new outrage in Belgium. New York Times, April 16, p. A4.

Gilgun, Jane F. (2011). By all means, do not renounce Satan and his evil works. http://www.scribd.com/doc/52492534/By-All-Means-Do-Not-Renounce-Satan-and-his-Evil-Works

Gilgun, Jane F. (2011). Perfect: The bishop has no shame. http://www.scribd.com/doc/53136862/Perfect-The-Bishop-Has-no-Shame

Gilgun, Jane F. (2010). Child sexual abuse: From harsh realities to hope. http://www.scribd.com/doc/16484981/Child-Sexual-Abuse-From-Harsh-Realities-to-Hope

Gilgun, Jane F. (2010). Evil feels good: Think before you act. http://www.scribd.com/doc/38489251/Evil-Feels-Good-Think-Before-You-Act

Gilgun, Jane F. (2010). Fake accountability & true: Telling the difference. http://www.scribd.com/doc/38241791/Fake-Accountability-True-Telling-the-Difference/

Gilgun, Jane F. (2010). On being a shit: Unkind deeds and cover-ups in everyday life. http://www.amazon.com/dp/B0015XV33Y

Gilgun, Jane F. (2010). Survivors of priest abuse told for 50 years: No one listened. http://www.scribd.com/doc/29020383/Survivors-of-Priest-Abuse-Told-for-50-Years-No-One-Listened

Gilgun, Jane F. (2010). Why they do it: Beliefs & emotional gratification lead to violent acts. http://www.scribd.com/doc/30778872/Why-They-Do-It-Beliefs-Emotional-Gratification-Lead-to-Violent-Acts ?The Diocese of Antigonish?http://www.antigonishdiocese.com/title.htm?. STATEMENTS regarding Raymond J. Lahey, former bishop of Antigonish, may be found at: The Canadian Conference of Catholic Bishops ?http://www.cccb.ca/site/eng?

The Vatican Press Office: ?http://www.vatican.va/news_services/press/vis/vis_en.html?

Afterword

The following is an example of what the pope and abusive priests can say. This is an excerpt from "Survivors of Priest Abuse Told for 50 Years: No one Listened."

Pope Benedict Has An Opportunity
to Bring About Major Change

In the past several years, Pope Benedict has changed. He has learned that Church policy was wrong. He has made many statements to that effect. He has expressed concern to survivors in personal meetings with them. He has said that Church actions of the past are shameful. Many, like me, do not think he has gone far enough, but he has come to realize that past policy led to hurts and wrongs.

Most religions are compassionate. We are taught to love the sinner but not the sin. We are taught to confess, to be fully accountable for our wrong-doings, to be contrite, to do penance, and to change our ways.

By his actions, Pope Benedict is a sinner along with the rest of us. He has an opportunity to be an international role model of accountability. He can make a full public confession of his sins on the steps of St. Peter's Church, in Rome, where he is the pastor. This is an example of what he can say.

I have been wrong about the sexual abuse of children. I have shown callous disregard for the well-being of children. I have allowed archbishops, bishops, cardinals, and other priests to show callous disregard for children. These actions are wrong. Sacrificing children for the sake of the Church's reputation is wrong. Showing mercy to abusing priests without accountability is wrong. I have committed grievous sins.

Child sexual abuse is an abuse of power. When priests sexually abuse children, they take advantage of Church teachings that priests are God's representatives on Earth. Children believe this. Priests tell children that sexual abuse is God's love and God wants children to learn about love and to be loving. This is a hideous distortion of Church teachings. Abusing priests have distorted Church teachings so that they can experience what they believe are the greatest feelings in the world, states of bliss and fulfillment, and bliss.

I have allowed priests to take advantage of children even after I learned that they were sexual abusers of children. I hope the Church faithful can forgive me. The faithful will see that every action I take from now on in regard to priest sexual abuse will be to show compassion for survivors and to make every human effort to prevent any child sexual abuse in the future.

The Pope can also advise cardinals, archbishops, bishops, and other priests who have been involved in protecting the Church and showing disregard for children to make similar public statements of accountability.

In addition, the Pope can institute policies where priests who have abused children in the past and any who are discovered to have sexually abused children to make full confessions on the steps of St. Peter's. This is an example of what these priests can say.

I was selfish and insensitive. I took advantage of my position as a priest. The children believed I was special. They believed I was God's representative on earth. The children were afraid to say no to me. I hurt them. I am sorry. I will do whatever I have to do to make sure I do not hurt any other children again. I abused my power. I knew deep down I had power over children and they would do what I wanted.

I did not care what the children wanted. I wanted the incredible pleasure I got from sexually abusing children. What children wanted and needed from me did not matter. All that mattered was what I wanted. I fooled myself into believing the children enjoyed the sex, but in my heart I knew better. The children wanted me to love then, but not in sexual ways. Children required my fond regard and guidance and not exploitation. Whatever abuse I experienced in the past is not excuse for my own abuse.

I betrayed my priestly vows. I am sorry. I will do whatever it takes to make up for the hurt I have caused. By my acts of sexual abuse, I have shown callous disregard for the welfare of children.

A Fairy Tale?

Are public statements of wrong-doings a fairy tale? A fantasy? Do the Pope, others responsible for not protecting children, and abusing priest truly believe Church doctrine? If they do, they will make full public confessions that are broadcast throughout the world. Showing how to be accountable can have an enormous impact for good.

Note: This article was first published in 2011.

5

Lust, Agape, Philia, & Erotic Love:
Meanings in Relationships

*The path to erotic or romantic love is through agape
and philia experienced with equals*

Reviewer: *"one not to get….relationships are built on trust."*

Lust is an overwhelming desire to be sexual with another person without forethought, including little or no thought about consequences for self or other. It's delightful to anticipate and blissful to experience, but mindless. Lust can lead to friendship and to agape, but it often leads to unhappy consequences for one or both involved.

Agape is love that involves the active promotion of the well being of the other. Agape is mindful. Agape also can be passionate in some ways, as when parents love children, but desire for sexual union is not part of agape. Agape is deeply satisfying and is a large component of what makes living meaningful.

Some people have a general attitude of agape toward others with whom they are in contact. It is a regard they give freely, without expectation of mutuality. In order to have this kind of agape, I would imagine that such individuals would also have relationships that are mutual, in order to refresh and replenish themselves.

Philia is friendship that is mutual, but also that is dependent upon circumstances. Persons who experience friendship often have shared interests. Typical friendships are between persons of equal power, but older people can be friends with younger people, if there is mutual respect for the differences associated with age, such as the power older people often have over younger people.

In many circumstances, it may not be possible for friendships to exist when one person has power over another, such as a professor being friends with students or bosses being friends with persons they supervise and have the power to hire and fire.

Friendship can combine with agape so that persons are friends with shared interests and who mutually promote the interests of others.

Erotic love is mindful and involves the active promotion of the well-being of others and   that involve the mutuality of friendships, in combination with a powerful desire to be sexual with a person who is of equal status and power. Erotic love is spiritual as well as deeply physical. It is difficult to tell where physicality ends and spirituality begins. The boundaries between physicality and spirituality are blurred. Some people say they are never more themselves and never more fulfilled than when they experience erotic love. Erotic love occurs between equals and is a form of romantic love.

Those who live in love live mostly in agape and in philia. How fortunate they are. Those who also experience erotic love experience it at various points in their lives, but not all day long every day, the way many people experience agape and philia.

At my age, I think about my younger selves and the good fortune I have had in terms of experiences of agape, philia, and erotic love. My experiences of lust were a series of bumbles and stumbles that taught me much. I may not have learned what I learned any other way. At the same time, a few words from my elders might have spared me unhappiness. I hope these words of mine help others to learn something about agape, philia, erotic love, and lust.

Agape and Erotic Love

I can't imagine a human being who does not want agape and philia, that delightful, light, and easy reciprocal connection of one person to another. Most of us experience this, possibly most or all of the time. Philia usually builds over time. There may be an attraction to someone, in the sense that one person feels comfortable with and interested in another person. This can lead to friendships and many kinds of meaningful activities. Friends talk about all kinds of things. They share activities. Friendship can become sacred spaces.

Any chance that another person will become best friends forever, however, requires agape as well as mutuality. Agape is the commitment to the well-being of another, and in friendship this is a mutual commitment.

Once in a while, friends who experience their being together as sacred spaces move toward erotic love. Certain conditions appear to be present when erotic love leads to good outcomes. These conditions include

• both persons are available, equal in status and power, and not committed to another person or to a path in life that excludes erotic relationships;

• both persons are gardeners for the other, cultivating each other over time, watering, sheltering from hail and frosts; their erotic love blooms as a flower does, gradually opening wider and wider in vibrant expectancy; and

• both persons are accountable for any hurtful actions they commit, take responsibility for their actions, recognize the harm they have caused, apologize, make amends, and do whatever it takes not to repeat the harmful actions.

Young people need to know that the path to erotic love is through agape, the active cultivation of friendships that involve of mutual care, fairness, and honesty. Fairness and honesty are important because disagreements and misattunements occur in agape-friendship combinations. That is why accountability and working at not repeating hurtful behaviors are central to relationships that are erotic in the way I mean them.

I recommend at least three instances of breakdowns and repair in relationship in order to trust that the mutuality, honesty, and fairness are lasting. In relationships on their way to erotic love, I recommend the same before giving in to the powerful sexual desire for the other. In other words, don't hop in the sack until you have experienced multiple instances of the above characteristics.

Building relationships of trust takes time. If you do hop in the sack without really knowing and trusting another, be prepared for a range of consequences. This is lust responding to lust, which is sometimes satisfying in the short and long run. It's a crap shoot, however. The odds favor hurt, regret, and guilt.

Mismatches Between Agape and Lust

Sometimes there is a mismatch between agape. Friendship, and lust. One person in a relationship may experience agape and friendship for another, while the other experiences lust. When this happens between adults of equal status, such situations may be handled well. The person being pursued says no, and the pursuer respects that boundary. In other situations, rather than accepting no for a response, some individuals insist on their own way and harass others sexually to get what they want. What they want is a satisfaction of their lust.

What pursuers want does not involve erotic love because they are uninterested in mutuality and in the promotion of the well-being of the other. Some may fool themselves into thinking the sex they want with the other is good for the other, but self-deception does not make such thinking true.

There are many situations where older persons, males and females, pretend to have agape and friendship when they only want to be sexual and don't think about what may happen to the other as a result of the sexual activity. I have seen this a lot in my research and in my professional practice as a social worker. For example, older teenage boys or young men do all they can to engage a younger girl in sexual relationships.

They dazzle her with their wit and charm, sweet talk, and promises. The girls and inexperienced young women think these boys and men really care or even love them. They think they are in love. They don't know that agape and friendship compose the road to erotic love, or the romantic love they crave. What they get is a brief involvement with someone who uses them and goes away. This is a mismatch between what the pursuer wants and what the target of his pursuit wants and gets.

This same kind of thing can happen when older boys and men have lust for younger boys and when older girls and women have lust for younger girls or boys. The pursuers want the gratification, satisfaction, bliss, and thrill of sexual contact with someone they lust after. Pursuers are either short-sighted or callous about consequences. Their targets may be too young, too afraid, or too flattered to understand what pursuers are asking of them. They may not see pursuers as the betrayers that they are.

No one has taught the targets of lust to know the differences between lust, agape, friendship, and erotic love. They had no idea the other wants to use them. The other person may see them as conquests whose acquiescence leads to bragging rights. These users puff themselves up at the expense of others and often seek to brag to an audience of like-minded users.

Some of those in lust have other motivations, including believing themselves to be in love. Whether they show agape comes out in how they treat the other after the sexual acts take place. In telling the difference between lust, agape, friendship, and erotic love, actions tell the truth, while feelings and words can lie, even when those in lust do not have these intentions.

Sometimes there is mutual lust, where two people hunger for each other sexually without really knowing each other. Each may have some kind of moral code that guides them to promote the well-being of others, to engage in mutual relationships, and to take good care of themselves. When in lust, however, concern for self and others flies away. What's left is bare naked lust. Sometimes people walk away from such experiences with happy memories, never to see the person again. Sometimes lust leads to love, and sometimes to heartbreak on one side or both.

Sometimes what appears to be lust is not lust, but the workings of a person's broken spirit, where the person mistakes the promise of sexual satisfaction for the satisfaction of friendship, mutual regard, and agape built upon romantic love. Some people are serial bed hoppers, seeking but not finding their one true love. Their task is to figure out how to heal their broken spirits, rebuild capacities for agape and for mutuality, and to avoid acting on their lust.

The harm that persons with broken spirits cause when they act on their lust is similar for those who act on lust out of the desire for a more simple kind of gratification. In other words, broken spirits or not, keep you hands to yourself and your knickers on and covered with outer garments.

Lust and Mismatches of Power

From the cradle to the grave those who have power over others require continual education about the limits of their power, the need to respect their power, and the importance of the promotion of the well-being of others, no matter how much they might want sexual satisfaction with others over whom they have authority. No matter what they think they are doing, they must not act on their desire for sexual and emotional gratification. They must think before they act. Evil feels good.

Lust that arises in relationships where one person has more power and authority than the other is always problematic. This can happen in relationships between supervisors and supervisees, teachers and students, parents and children, children and other children, and clergy with adult and child members of a faith community. Any individual with power over others and has any desire, no matter how small, to be sexual with subordinates must seek immediate counsel and ensure that they never are alone with the object of their lust.

Thousands of books and articles are available on these topics. Each instance of lust that is acted upon in power relationships is damaging to the targets. Children typically love their parents. Members of faith communities may respect and feel agape and friendship for clergy, and the same may be so for students in regard to their teachers and supervisees for their supervisors.

Sometimes persons in authority don't realize that they are abusing their authority. They may experience what they think is erotic love and swear ever-lasting devotion. They may tell their subordinates that this is love, as one man did as he sexually used his two year-old daughter or as priests and other clergy do when they abuse children or adult parishioners who go to them for pastoral counseling. Such individuals have huge gaps in their moral reasoning. They do not know the differences between, lust, agape, friendship, and erotic love.

Persons, including children, may be flattered beyond words at the attention of those whom they respect and for whom they have regard. They may experience sexual arousal themselves. Knowing the difference between lust, agape, philia, and erotic love may help many people in such situations to escape the worst of the potential damage the behaviors caused by the lustful desires of those who have authority over them.

I have one more small but final point about the terms, *lust, agape, philia*, and *erotic love*. *Lust* is an old-fashioned term. No one ever told me what it means and how it feels. I had no idea how good it feels and how powerful the pull to act on it. I couldn't think of another word that fits the idea that a person can want to be sexual with another without regard for the well-being of the targets or the longer term well-being of themselves.

Agape is a Greek word that means charity or care for others. It's rarely used, but I could think of no other word that means what agape means. The term *philia* means friendship as a form of love. The city of Philadelphia, means the city of brotherly love The term *erotic love* is probably old-fashioned and rarely used, but my sense of the term is that erotic love is transcendent love that is also sexual, possibly rare but based upon mutual regard and the mutual promotion of the well-being of the other.

Discussion

Erotic or romantic love builds upon agape and friendship between equals. Agape is the active promotion of the welfare of others of any age, and it may be one-way, regard offered with no expectation of return. Philia at its best is probably a form of agape, but it is a mutual kind of active promotion of the well-being of others. In combination, philia and agape represent a pathway toward erotic love when both persons have equal status and power. Persons who are equal in status and power and who act on mutual lust engage in a crap shoot. Sometimes mutual lust leads to friendship and then to erotic love, but most of the time it leads to unhappy consequences for one or both. Adults who take chances on lust also accept the consequences of acting on their sexual pull toward another.

Mismatches, when one person feels lust and the other agape, sometimes can be handled with simple boundary setting. Situations get more complicated when the pursuer in lust pretends to experience agape and the target trusts the pursuer. Rarely are the consequences anything but hurtful for the pursued and often for the pursuer as well.

Acting on lust when one person has authority over another is always wrong and always has hurtful consequences for the pursued and sometimes for the pursuer. Persons who act on their lust toward those with less power and who may even be dependent upon them have gaps in their moral reasoning. Their behaviors always damage the targets of their lust.

From cradle to grave, persons must be socialized to understand and respect the similarities and differences between lust, agape, and erotic love. They must be socialized to run as fast as they can for counsel when the delights of lust tickle their fancies, especially if the object of their lust has less power than they and may also be dependent upon them.

Thanks to Rev. Dr. Heidi Heidi Joos for speaking about philia. I and not Heidi am responsible for any misstatements in this article.

References

Buber, Martin (1937/2004). *I and thou.* London: Continuum.

Fromm, Erich (1956/2008). *The art of loving.* New York: Continuum.

Gilgun, Jane F. (2010). Child sexual abuse: From harsh realities to hope. http://www.scribd.com/doc/16484981/Child-Sexual-Abuse-From-Harsh-Realities-to-Hope

Gilgun, Jane F. (2010). Evil feels good: Think before you act. http://www.scribd.com/doc/38489251/Evil-Feels-Good-Think-Before-You-Act

Gilgun, Jane F. (2010). Nujood Ali, 10, divorces 30 year-old husband. http://www.scribd.com/doc/27894576/Nujood-Ali-10-Divorces-her-30-Year-Old-Husband

Gilgun, Jane F. (2011). Original sin is not original, but goodness is. http://www.scribd.com/doc/49564877/Original-Sin-is-Not-Original-Goodness-is

Gilgun, Jane F. (2010). Parishioners express outrage at survivors of priest abuse. http://www.scribd.com/doc/30474916/Parishioners-Express-Outrage-at-SURVIVORS-of-Priest-Abuse

Gilgun, Jane F. (2010). Survivors of priest abuse told for 30 years; No one listened. http://www.scribd.com/doc/29020383/Survivors-of-Priest-Abuse-Told-for-50-Years-No-One-Listened

6

Marly, 12: A Bright Future if Only....

Reviewer: *"a waste of time"*

Marly is a 12 year-old girl with a lot going for her, but also with a lot working against her. She is attractive, bright, and personable. Other people like her. She and her mother have been receptive to intensive social services for almost three years. When in situations where she is comfortable, Marly excels. When she is stressed, Marly becomes physically aggressive and verbally abusive. Her aggressive behaviors mirror the aggression she has witnessed in her family, where she has seen her mother react aggressively when upset and where she has seen her mother's partner physically abuse her mother from the time she was a toddler.

School administrators have suspended Marly for fighting many times, and she has changed schools about eight times in the six years she has been in school. This article is a portrait of Marly. Its purpose is to show how a great little girl is up against forces she can neither understand nor cope with unless many others provide her with the resources required for her to do so. This is a descriptive case study. In the discussion, I suggest that the NEATS assessment is useful in the analysis of the descriptive material in the case study, with special emphasis on how race-based issues and racism have affected Marly's development and life chances.

Gail had high hopes for Marly. For 18 months, Gail had been Marly's case manager in the EXCEL program, a county-based social service agency whose goal is to promote the optimal functioning of children growing up under adverse conditions. This is what Gail said about Marly's situation a little more than a year ago. I interviewed Gail as part of long-term research I have conducted with EXCEL. I had asked Gail to talk about a case that is going well.

> I'm really happy with Marly, my young girl. She is 11 and in the fifth grade in a suburban school. I wouldn't say that Marly necessarily is stable, but the reason I'm happy with that case is because I have an excellent relationship with her mom, the school, her therapist, and herself. I think there is a lot of good communication between all parties. I feel like mom trusts me and

trusts my advice and comes to me for advice for situations with Marly. Mom lets me give my honest opinion. I'm able to say, 'This isn't working. You've got to try something different.'

I think that developed because for a long time, I didn't give my opinion. I just kind of let mom talk and bounced back to her what she said to me and helped her process things. She would come up with stuff on her own. Once she got comfortable talking to me and trusted me more, it was easier for me then to interject some advice, whatever you want to call it, counseling.

Marly's been at three different schools since I've worked with her. I've just gotten really lucky that the staff at the school communicate with me really well. The school's she's at now--I was initially really nervous for her to go there because that would be the first time in a suburban school setting, so different from the urban schools she's been in. She's going to be in a segregated special education classroom. I was really, really worried. She's African American. The school is majority Caucasian.

I had a lot of concerns, but it actually turned out to be pretty good for her because a lot of the issues she has are similar to issues that kids with autism have. She's got a lot of sensory stuff. She's triggered by too much noise and loud voices and all that stuff. So the small classroom size, which was, I think, based on an autism type model, is working really well for her. The teachers there are much more open to trying different ways to help her regulate herself. For example, her therapist bought her a jewelry making kit. Marly's really, really good at anything, you know, hand motor skills. She likes arts and crafts. She likes jewelry making. She likes knitting, all that stuff.

So her therapist had bought her a jewelry making kit and said she wanted me to talk to the teachers about her being able to use it at school to help regulate herself, because she has these explosive episodes at school. At that time she was at an urban school, and they were like, well, ok, we'll let her try, but it never happened. The learning centers have this policy. They stick to that policy. That's what they do.

At the suburban school, though, they were like, oh my God, tell her to bring the jewelry making kit in, anything that helps her. They're totally willing to individualize regulatory stuff to her personality. So, even though she's still having explosive episodes, they're fewer. They don't last as long. She's more willing to process through them afterwards.

Mom still has her dysfunctions, but she doesn't hide them from me. So, it's easier for me to work with them and know exactly what I'm dealing with. I'm sure mom isn't completely open with me. There's definitely stuff that I don't know about, but mom doesn't hide from me that she drinks. She doesn't hide from me that she is physical with her kids sometimes. So because she can trust to talk to me about those things, I feel like I can have more of an impact on mom's parenting.

Seven months after this interview, Gail left EXCEL. Justine took over Gail's caseload as case manager. Justine continued to be effective in maintaining working relationships with the various persons in Marly's life.

A year after the interview with Gail, Marly was locked up in a juvenile detention center. She had been with three other girls who jumped a woman on the street, beat the woman up, and stole her purse as part of an initiation into a girl's gang. The women fell to the sidewalk and hit her head on a curb. She had a concussion but no skull fracture. Marly allegedly did not touch the woman, but she was there. Someone recognized Marly and reported her to the police who arrested Marly. Brought into juvenile court on felony assault charges, the judge sentenced Marly to 30 days in juvenile detention. Marly did not identify the other two girls, one of whom reported on Facebook, "I did something, and somebody else is going down for it." Marly could not "snitch."

The 30-day sentence upset the carefully coordinated systems of relationships that Gail helped to create and that Justine maintained. Suddenly, Marly was no longer part of a system of persons who cared about her. The apparent shock of Marly's sentence upset her mother Nikki to the point where she was of no help to Marly. Justine reported, "The mom is a drinker.... She just walked out of court. When the judge said they were holding Marly, the mother left, talking crazy."

Like Gail, Justine has hopes for Marly, whom she sees as alternating between being a little girl, a leader, and a pre-teen involved in antisocial peer groups. She said, "The day she told me she was in a gang, we had seen the Toy Story 3, a total kids' movie. It's the cutest darn movie. Marly loved it. Sometimes she's a total kid. After the movie, she told me she was in a girls' gang. I asked her, 'What did you do? Have sex with those boys?' I just flat out asked her. 'No,' she said. 'I just took licks from the girls.' They jumped her, and they fought her."

Justine reported on what Marly thought about being in a gang and how she, Justine, views Marly and her situation.

She thought it was cute. She smiled. 'Yeah, I'm a lady gang member.' When I dropped her off, I had a feeling....The incident happened the very next day. She's a tough one. She's a really good kid. She's got a future if she can just pull it together. I see her at the

JDC almost every day. Every time I see her, she cries....She's a bright, bright girl. She gets it. She says things that you would think are far past her understanding.... She's got that temper. Her mom's got that temper. Her mom and her, the relationship is more like friends. The mother used to use physical punishment, but it didn't look like physical punishment because she is a small woman....

Justine had more to say about Marly.

>She had been doing really well in the girls group I'm leading. She's a leader. The girls look up to her. She's got potential to be somebody. That's why it's so hard. It's like it's all stacked against her. This is how your mom handles conflict. This is how your mom handles anything that goes wrong. She's yelling. She's in the hallway yelling at the public defender at court.

Information From Records

According to school and social service records, Marly is cute, personable, and smart. Other people like her, including children, her teachers, and social service providers. School records state that she thrives on individual attention and "gets along with everyone when she is not angry." She gets mostly A's on her report card. She is in special education classes at school for children with emotional and behavioral problems and not for academic difficulties. She becomes physically and verbally aggressive when she believes other children disrespect her. She is aggressive in the classroom, in hallways, in the lunchroom, on the playground, on the school bus, and at the school bus stop.

Marly has never physically injured anyone, but she punches, pulls hair, threatens others verbally, and curses. She has attended eight schools in six years, both because her family moves and because school personnel think she will do better elsewhere. Her 32 year-old mother Nikki yells and hangs up when school personnel phone about Marly's behaviors. Nikki does not attend school meetings about Marly. As she said to Justine, "Why bother? They don't listen to me anyway."

In many ways, Marly mirrors Nikki's behaviors and the behaviors she has observed between her mother and her mother's long-term partner, Reginald. Both have arrests for domestic assault, physical assault in the community, weapons and drug charges. Both have served time in jail and the workhouse, while Reginald has been in prison and the workhouse several times for six months to two years at a time. Nikki and Reginald were under child protection supervision for 18 months when Marly was between the ages of nine and 10. Neither adult complied with the case plan. Child protection closed the case anyway.

Nikki has a measured IQ of about 70, but social service records suggest that she tests low because she has a learning disability related to reading and is often agitated when taking written tests. They believe she is very intelligent. Because of her low tested IQ, Nikki's sources of income include disability payments and welfare payments for her children. Marly is the oldest. Marly has one full brother Marcus who is a year younger. Their father is Nikki's former husband who is in prison on drug and attempted murder charges. Nikki has one other child, a son, with Reginald. The youngest child is three. Nikki had a tubal ligation when this child was born.

Marcus, too, gets suspended frequently for fighting. His grades are mostly Cs, but he is not in a resource room because he fights less frequently than Marly and appears not to have sensory issues. Yet, Marly gets into some of Marcus's fights because she sticks up for her younger brother. Sometimes Marly and Marcus are suspended from school at the same time because they were involved in the same fight.

Early Family History

Nikki was in a shelter when Marly was a toddler and Marcus an infant. Records at the shelter noted that Nikki was verbally and physically abusive toward Marly. Staff were concerned that Nikki also hit Marcus and picked him up and carried him around by the wrist. A staff person wrote, "Mom is not working with staff at shelter. She remains very uninvolved." The records noted an incident where Nikki was playing a computer game when a staff person asked her to change Marly's diaper. Nikki became angry, snatched her child from the floor, and plunked her on a couch. She turned back to her game. The staff person changed Marly's diaper. She wrote, "I observed the diaper being very soiled and apparently not changed for some time."

Another part of the record noted that when staff asked Nikki not to hit Marly, Nikki said, "No one is going to tell her how to fucking raise her child." The shelter staff called the police and filed a report of abuse. The record noted that if the staff observe any more abuse, "the children are subject to placement in alternative care."

Marly in Grade School

Marly missed 60 days of first grade. In response, a school attendance officer made a home visit. Nikki said her partner Reginald beat her so badly a few months earlier that she now has an order for protection against him. In addition, Marcus had been hyperactive to the point where she doesn't know what to do with her. She said she had been working on getting computer training at a community college. She is having a hard time getting anyone to watch her toddler son Tone who is not in school. As for the school attendance, she said she had been out of town. Marly had been staying with her paternal grandmother in a neighboring town. The grandmother had not gotten Marly to school.

Nikki said Marly has been in trouble on the bus for fighting and doesn't like to ride it anymore. She gets out of bed in the morning, then dawdles, and doesn't want to get dressed. She said she needs an alarm clock, doesn't want counseling, and doesn't need anything from social services.

The attendance officer explained what would happen as school personnel proceeded with the truancy hearing. The attendance officer talked to Nikki about a case plan, and she said she already had one. Nikki said she was arrested recently because the police thought she had shot a gun at a neighbor. The police questioned her, but did not arrest her. She also said she had been in jail over the weekend. A friend, who is living with her, accused Nikki of hitting her. Nikki said she had not.

The officer asked why Marly and Marcus were home from school that day. Nikki said Marly was kicked off the bus. Nikki said Marly had been suspended from school last week. Another girl had gotten a little paint on her, and Marly threw paint at the other little girl. Nikki said both girls were suspended from school for one day.

The county filed a CHIPS petition on Marly on the basis of educational neglect. Nikki admitted the neglect. The court ordered county protective supervision which it maintained for 18 months, with no change in Marly's attendance. Overall, Nikki and her partner Reginald did not fulfill the terms of the case plan, as mentioned earlier.

A few months later, Nikki was in the hospital with a compound fracture to her left arm and a skull fracture. She said it was a domestic. She was scheduled for brain surgery. The day before her surgery, the case record noted that a social worker had visited with Nikki in the hospital. Nikki said that Marly was doing well in school. She had a new teacher and likes her. Nikki's mother was staying with the children and getting them to school.

Incident That Led to EXCEL Referral

When Marly was in the third grade, she got into a fight with another girl. The girl had bumped into her in the intervention room where both girls were because their classroom teacher wanted both of them to have a timeout. Marly bumped her back. They got into a fistfight that spilled out into the hallway. The teacher and assistant principal pulled the girls apart. The assistant principal escorted Marly to his office. On the way, Marly yelled, "Bitch, I'm going to kill you. That's not a threat. That's a fucking promise." According to the principal, Marly called the other girl a "fucking bitch" six times. The principal made a police report.

The police referred Marly and her family to EXCEL. The agency accepted the family for services. Gail became her case manager. With some hesitancy at first, Nikki accepted services. Gail worked at building relationships with the various people involved with Marly and with Nikki and the rest of her family.

EXCEL provides intensive services to families with children who have experienced adverse circumstances, who have few resources, and who have a child or children in trouble with the law before the age of ten. The purpose of EXCEL is to provide services and resources that promote optimal child and family development and that keep children from involvement in the juvenile justice system. Each case manager works with 14 families.

EXCEL has learned over the years that children do well in the program under several general conditions: 1) parents do all they can to become emotionally available to their children and provide structure, consistency, and love, 2) service providers understand the children's and families' challenging issues and behaviors and have the training and resources to respond competently, 3) case managers form working alliances with the children, their parents, and other service providers, 4) the multiple service providers who typically work with the families coordinate their services, and 5) children engage in activities they enjoy and in which they do well.

Many parents are unable to deal with the issues that interfere with their emotional availability and other capacities for parenting. Services often are disjointed and inadequate. Service providers appear not to understand the children and family and respond in ways that may be unhelpful. Case managers may be unable to form working alliances with the children, their parents, or both children and parents.

The best outcomes appear to occur when these five elements are in play. Children can avoid involvement in correctional systems and do quite well in school and community when some of these elements are lacking, but child working alliances with case managers and children engaging in activities where they experience mastery, competence, and enjoyment appear to be necessary for this to happen in the relative absence of parental availability and competence and service provision competence.

An Example of Marly's Challenging Behaviors

The following is an example of challenging behaviors that Marly has shown during the years she has been under the scrutiny of social services. One spring morning, about 18 months ago, Gail went to Marly's school to drive her to therapy. Marly was ten years old. This is what Gail reported.

> A school staff member tried to get Marly's attention in the cafeteria. Marly did not notice because she was yelling and cursing at a teacher. She walked by me in a huff to leave the cafeteria. I grabbled her hand to stop her, but she jerked her and away from me and kept walking. I followed her into the intervention room. She was crying and angry. The other staff got on the phone and was talking to someone, saying that Marly was out of control. I hugged her really tight and whispered to her to calm down. We walked out of intervention. I told staff that I would be bring her to therapy. Marly held onto me until we left school. I talked to her in the car about being able to calm herself down. I also talked to her about how the teachers are labeling her a bad kid because of her behavior.

A few weeks later, Gail's toddler was sick. She called Nikki to tell her she could not take Marly to therapy. Nikki said she couldn't either because her car was in the shop. Gail asked a neighbor to care for her son. Gail transported Marly to therapy.

A few days later, Marly hit another girl whom she said had stolen pencils from her desk. The principal sent her to the intervention room, which a teacher's aide supervises and which has unbreakable soft toys for the children to play with. Marly asked to phone her mother. The aide refused. Marly left the school and called the police who came to the school immediately. Marly denied calling the police. The school social worker told Gail that the vice principal is "considering this is Marly's last chance."

Marly is presently at a turning point in her life. She still has opportunities to do well in school, family, and community, but she has a lot of cope with. Her mother Nikki wants Marly to do well, but her mother also is unable to deal with her own issues regarding aggression, her alcohol use, and other counter-productive behaviors, as her recent actions in court show.

Summary & Discussion

Marly is a 12 year-old African American child who is intelligent, personable, and attractive. For most children, these personal assets predict a happy future. Marly, however, contends with multiple adverse circumstances that undermine her life chances. Social service records document complex traumas that Marly has experienced throughout her life with little evidence of helpful social service intervention. These traumas are related to homelessness, parental criminality, child protection involvement, parental use of alcohol, and parental arrests for partner violence, as well as frequent and unpredictable absences of both mother and mother's partners from the family home because of incarceration and hospitalization for physical injury.

Marly shows similar physical and verbal aggression that her mother and other parental figures show. In addition, Marly has sensory integration issues that appear to increase her volatility. For example, she has a younger brother Marcus who does not have sensory issues. Marcus is less frequently volatile than Marly, although Marcus gets into fights with other children. Because of her behavioral issues, Marly is a student in a small, contained classroom while Marcus is not.

Marly has experienced at least eight changes of schools in five years and is routinely subject so school suspensions. Within the past few months, she joined a girls' gang. Police arrested her when she was part of a small group of girls who beat, robbed, and injured a woman waiting at the bus stop. This action was part of an initiation of one of the other girls into the gang. She presently is incarcerated in juvenile detention. Her mother has reacted in angry and avoidant ways and has been unable to be of support to Marly during this difficult time.

The EXCEL program case managers developed good working relationships with Marly, Nikki, and the several professionals involved in Marly's life. As is shown in the case description, however, the persons involved in this web of relationships sometimes added to Marly's stress. Examples are Nikki storming out of the courtroom and the assistant principal counting the number of times Marly cursed rather than attempting to connect with Marly to guide her toward more prosocial ways of expressing displeasure.

Thus, Marly's support system was imperfect, but there was reason to hope, given her positive personal qualities and the fact that there was a coordinated system in which she was embedded. The felony assault and subsequent incarceration in juvenile detention catapulted Marly out of this web of relationships into an environment in which she is unlikely to thrive.

The case study is primarily descriptive, attempting to present the circumstances of a young person's life in the settings in which she participates. For the most part, I avoided using language that stands for explicit concepts related to five areas that research has established as fundamental to human development. These five areas are neurobiology, executive function, attachment, trauma, and self-regulation.

Researchers and practitioners have documented that child and family development in these five areas takes place in various social contexts that involve multiple influences, including contemporaneous, historical, and developmental. For example, I could interpret Marly's aggressive behaviors and pride in participating in a girl's gang as an outcome related to several of the areas of the NEATS, such as attachment and related concepts of inner working models, executive function which connects to brain development and capacities for self-regulation and anticipating consequences, and trauma, which can shape brain development, inner working models, and capacities for attachment, executive function, and self-regulation. Think in terms of the social context in which Marly has lived her life, and I could then discuss the possible effects of poverty, homelessness, racism, community violence, and social policies and programs that appear to have been ineffective in providing Marly's families with the resources required to provide a safe, stable, and loving home.

Marly's situation is typical in child welfare caseloads. Poor, young African American families are disproportionately represented in public child welfare. Talented, personable, and intelligent young people like Marly find life circumstances overwhelming with few resources and consistent care that children require to thrive. A deeper and broader approach to Marly's situation would go beyond description to analysis. The NEATS assessment, which incorporates the ideas just discussed, is a starting point for the analysis. Such an assessment requires careful attention to risks and resources, including how Marly and her family have experienced issues related to race and racism.

References

Gilgun, Jane F. (2011). Jacinta's lament. http://www.scribd.com/doc/58391990/Jacinta's-Lament-Happy-Father-s-Day-Dad or http://www.amazon.com/Jacintas-Lament-Happy-Fathers-ebook/dp/B00579YDB6/ref=sr_1_1?s=digital-text&ie=UTF8&qid=1314812287&sr=1-1

Gilgun, Jane F. (2011). *The NEATS: A child and family assessment.* Amazon.

Lieberman, Alicia F. (2007). Ghosts and angels: Intergenerational patterns in the transmission and treatment of the traumatic sequelae of domestic violence. *Infant Mental Health Journal, 28(3),* 422-439.

Zeanah, Charles H., Jr. (Ed.) (2009). *Handbook of infant mental health* (3rd ed.). New York: Guilford.

7

Preliminary Studies
and Qualitative Research

Reviewer: *"not helpful....very dissatisfied"*

When considering a study using qualitative methods, it is important to do preliminary exploration of your topic. Besides reading about your topic, you can do this through talking to knowledgeable people, such as friends, professionals, and others who have some experience with your topic.

Preliminary studies are probably necessary for proposal writing, in particular proposals you are planning to submit for funding. Strauss (1987) was explicit about this. He wrote, "No proposal should be written without preliminary data collection and analysis" (p. 286).

If you do preliminary studies, you will develop a focus, which is essential early in qualitative research, even though the purpose of many projects is to develop new understandings. In addition, preliminary studies will help you formulate questions that are stated in language that research participants will understand and experience as natural.

Few dissertation committees will allow PhD students to proceed with their research without a clear conceptual framework and carefully stated research goals and procedures. Preliminary studies are necessary to do this. Finally, institutional review boards that oversee the ethical component of research will not approve studies that are vague in purpose, focus, and procedures.

The notion of preliminary studies is consistent with the work of Glaser and Strauss (1967). On the one hand, Glaser and Strauss recommended entering the field with no hypotheses to test and to see what emerges. This leads many researchers new to qualitative research to assume that these methodologists are stating that it is unnecessary to do prior literature reviews and to plan out research procedures before the study begins. On the other hand, Glaser and Strauss also acknowledged in a footnote that researchers are not blank slates and bring their pre-conceptions with them.

Elizabeth Bott

Elizabeth Bott (1957) may have been one of the inspirations for Glaser and Strauss's (1967) thinking. She and her research team identified and elaborated upon the notion of social network through entering the field with no hypotheses to test. Yet, Bott also stated that her general conceptual framework was Lewin's ecological theory, which sensitized her to the notion of social networks. Schatzman (in Gilgun, 1993) discussed a similar phenomenon when a research team headed by Anselm Strauss identified and elaborated the term "negotiated order" (Strauss et al, 1964).

Thus, qualitative research may well begin with no hypotheses to test but as soon as researchers identify concepts and processes that they want to elaborate, they engage in a kind of testing. Glaser and Strauss (1967) call this the constant comparative method, where they compare their findings within and across cases and modify their hypotheses to fit their findings. They identify new cases through theoretical sampling, which involves choosing cases on the basis of the promise they hold to elaborate upon or refine their emerging findings.

Analytic Induction

Constant comparison and theoretical sampling are similar to procedures of analytic induction, which begins with a conceptual model such as one or more preliminary hypotheses, sometimes simply a rough hypothesis or hunch based on intuition, and then seeks to test and elaborate upon this conceptual model.

Analytic induction tests and develops preliminary models/hypotheses through negative case analysis, a procedure that directs researchers to seek cases that may undermine emerging findings. If the new cases do this, the conceptual model is reformulated and modified. In this way, researchers develop findings that account for and document general patterns and exceptions to the patterns.

Since few qualitative studies have random samples, qualitative findings can tell us little or anything about prevalence but it can tell us a great deal about variations in patterns and meanings. Finally, analytic induction is not "pure" induction, just as grounded theory is not (Gilgun, 2002).

Students and new researchers often are confused about the place of preliminary hypotheses in qualitative research. It is little wonder. Major figures such as Glaser and Strauss (1967; Strauss & Corbin, 1998) are unclear. In the final analysis, preliminary studies are good practice, with full acknowledgement that researchers' prior notions shape their views of which phenomena are important. Once researchers identify the focus of their research, they are then positioned to do a literature review, develop a conceptual framework, set out goals of their research, and plan procedures of data collection and analysis.

Negative case analysis, which involves the conscious choosing of cases that will force modification and sometimes even refutation of emerging findings, is key to qualitative analysis. Many new researchers are tempted to see only what their conceptual models says is important. By directing researchers to seek material that will challenge their models, researchers are positioned to develop new understandings. It's easy to find material that supports prior frameworks. The skill of qualitative analysis is to challenge prior understandings so new meanings can emerge.

Discussion

Preliminary studies solve many problems. Ph.D. students who require the permission of committees to go forward with the research must have a focus and literature reviews. Researchers seeking funding have to be specific about what they want to do research on. If they do preliminary studies, they will have a focus around which they can develop their review of the literature. Preliminary studies provide a way of finding an innovative focus. What's not to like about preliminary studies? They do take time, but the rewards are worth it.

References

Bott, Elizabeth (1957). *Family and social network.* New York: Free Press. Second edition published in 1971.

Gilgun, Jane F. (2002). Conjectures and refutations: Governmental funding and qualitative research. *Qualitative Social Work, 1(3),* 359-375.

Gilgun, Jane F. (1993). Dimensional analysis and grounded theory: An interview with Leonard Schatzman. *Qualitative Family Research, 7 (1 &2),* 1-2, 4-7.

Gilgun, Jane F. (2012). Enduring themes in qualitative family research. *Journal of Family Theory and Review,* 4, 80-95.

Gilgun, Jane F. & Roberta G. Sands (in press). Special issue editorial: The contribution of qualitative approaches to developmental intervention research. *Qualitative Social Work: Research and Practice.*

Gilgun, Jane F. (2010). Reflections on 25 years of research on violence. *Reflections: Narratives of Professional Helping,* 16(4), 50-59.

Gilgun, Jane F. (2006). The four cornerstones of qualitative research. *Qualitative Health Research, 16(3),* 436-443.

Gilgun, Jane F. (2005). Qualitative research and family psychology.

Journal of Family Psychology,19(1), 40-50.

Popper, Karl R. (1969). *Conjectures and refutations: The growth of scientific knowledge.* London: Routledge and Kegan Paul.

Strauss, Anselm (1987). *Qualitative analysis for social scientists.* New York: Cambridge University Press.

Strauss, Anselm, & Juliet Corbin (1998). *Basics of qualitative research: Techniques and procedures for developing grounded theory* (2nd ed.). Thousand Oaks, CA: Sage.

Strauss, Anselm, Leonard. Schatzman, Rue Bucher, Danuta Ehrlich, & Marvin Sabshin (1964). *Psychiatric ideologies and institutions.* New York: Free Press.

Note: Written in 2003. I did minor editing in May 2012.

8

Survivors of Priest Abuse Told for 50 Years:
No One Listened

Reviewer: *"a rip off...says it's 133 pages"*

For 50 years, deaf boys at a church-run school in Wisconsin used every possible means to tell everyone possible that Lawrence Murphy, a priest who was first a teacher and then head of the school, was sexually abusing them. NO ONE STOPPED MURPHY. Murphy was at the school for 24 years, from 1950 to 1974. Boys reported the abuse the entire time. They told their parents, other priests, three archbishops in Milwaukee who were Murphy's supervisors, district attorneys, and police. Their parents were solidly behind them. Not only was Murphy promoted to be head of the school, he was buried in full priestly garments when he died in 1998. He abused at least 200 boys.

The present head of the Roman Catholic Church, Pope Benedict, showed mercy to Murphy in 1996 when he declined to expel Murphy from the priesthood. The Pope was then Cardinal Joseph Ratzinger, head of the Congregation of the Doctrine of the Faith, the Church structure that decides the fate or erring priests. Mercy is fine, even for child molesters, but accountability is important. A full public confession would have been right and proper. Think of the children who would not have been sexually abused if Cardinal Ratzinger had imposed that penance on Murphy. Penance is what Catholics do when they confess their sins and are "heartly sorry," in the words of the Act of Contrition, which is a prayer that follows confession of sins.

Murphy and the RC Church did nothing to repair the damage. Instead, the Church patriarchs cloaked the incident in as much secrecy as they could, abused their power, and did nothing to comfort the survivors who suffered their entire lives. Most if not all of the survivors felt shamed and guilty. They believed deep down that the abuse was their fault and that they are damaged goods. Cardinal Ratzinger showed no mercy for them.

The Horror

Murphy used his power as a priest not only to abuse children but to keep them quiet. He told the boys that God wanted him to teach them about sex, but the boys must keep the sex quiet because the sex took place under the seal of confession. Hideous. This is a hideous distortion of Church teaching and hideous abuse of power.

Within the RC Church, children are taught from an early age that priests are God's representatives on earth. They are links between ordinary people and God. When Catholics go to confession, they talk to God through priests. When priests say Mass, God is there on the altar. Children hold priests in awe. They can do no wrong.

Child molesters report that sex with children is "bliss," "the greatest feeling in the world," "thrills," "chills," and "deep and eternal love." Murphy may have felt that way about his sexual abuse of children. Something powerful impelled him to abuse his power as a priest. He knew that he was powerful in the eyes of children. He took advantage of his position and of children's awe of him. Horrific.

Will They Ever Learn?

Revelations of sexual abuse and cover-ups that go to the top of the Church hierarchy including more than one pope are bankrupting churches in many countries and are driving Catholics away from the church in droves. Murphy's case is one in a long line of cover-ups that clergy have perpetrated.

The case of John Geohgan, a priest in Boston, is similar to Murphy's case. Geoghan, however, was dismissed from the priesthood and died in prison. Geohgan abused about 130 boys for about 30 years in the Boston, Massachusetts, area. Records show that Cardinal Bernard Law, head of the church in the Boston area, first knew of Geoghan's sexually abusive behaviors the first year he was appointed Cardinal, 22 years before Geoghan was removed as a priest. Church authorities sent Geoghan to treatment many times, where he was declared cured. Then he was sent back to parishes, without informing the pastors of the parishes, where Geoghan abused boys again. He sometimes prayed as he molested the boys.

Parents, family members, and survivors wrote letters to church officials imploring them to do something. These letters were part of the court records at a civil trial where adult survivors received millions of dollars in damages. Cardinal Law retired as head of the Boston-area Church as a result of his mishandling of the Geoghan abuse case.

It is hard to understand how church authorities could allow sexually abusing priests to have on-going contact with children. Despite their spiritual authority, they apparently did not understand what child sexual abuse is, how it affects survivors, and that people they know and trust—even those they believe were called by God to be priests—would continue to abuse children after they received treatment, confessed their sins, and promised to stop.

Children as Collateral Damage

In Murphy's case and so many others, Church officials may have been doing damage control. They did not want to damage the credibility of the Church. Millions of people throughout the world look to the church for spiritual meaning and guidance. The Church has hundreds of billions of dollars in real estate. Church officials wanted to protect themselves and their view of the Church at all costs.

Children were collateral damage. Nothing excuses their lack of concern for children and inaction on their behalf. Only now did Pope Benedict offer apologies and express shame in his letter to the Catholics of Ireland, but he did so after years of publicity about these cover-ups of child sexual abuse and their unconscionable lack of concern for survivors.

Callous Disregard as Psychopathy

This callous disregard fits the definition of psychopathy.
Church authorities may have believed or wanted to believe that treatment, reprimand, repentance, and transfer to a new parish were enough. They might have seen only the many wonderful qualities these priests had and could not believe that such good men could abuse children sexually.

The priests could have been like other perpetrators, thinking they were doing no harm, that they were loving the children, and that they were entitled to a little pleasure because of all they gave up to be priests in the first place.

Still, the suspicion that Church officials were protecting the Church's reputation is a strong explanation for these cover-ups. The hypocrisy is hard to take in. The guardians of what is right and just, these representatives of God on earth, have done terrible things.

Pope Benedict Has An Opportunity
to Bring About Major Change

In the past several years, Pope Benedict has changed. He has learned that past Church policy was wrong. He has made many statements to that effect. He has expressed concern to survivors in personal meetings with them. He has said that Church actions of the past are shameful. Many, like me, do not think he has gone far enough, but he has come to realize that past policy led to hurts and wrongs.

Most religions are compassionate. We are taught to love the sinner but not the sin. We are taught to confess, to be fully accountable for our wrong-doings, to be contrite, to do penance, and to change our ways.

By his actions, Pope Benedict is a sinner along with the rest of us. He has an opportunity to be an international role model of accountability. He can make a full public confession of his sins on the steps of St. Peter's Church, in Rome, where he is the pastor. This is an example of what he can say.

> I have been wrong about the sexual abuse of children. I have shown callous disregard for the well-being of children. I have allowed archbishops, bishops, cardinals, and other priests to show callous disregard for children. These actions are wrong. Sacrificing children for the sake of the Church's reputation is wrong. Showing mercy to abusing priests without accountability is wrong. I have committed grievous sins.
>
> Child sexual abuse is an abuse of power. When priests sexually abuse children, they take advantage of Church teachings that priests are God's representatives on Earth. Children believe this. Priests tell children that sexual abuse is God's love and God wants children to learn about love and to be loving. This is a hideous distortion of Church teachings. Abusing priests have distorted Church teachings so that they can experience what they believe are the greatest feelings in the world, states of bliss and fulfillment, and bliss.
>
> I have allowed priests to take advantage of children even after I learned that they were sexual abusers of children. I hope the Church faithful can forgive me. The faithful will see that every action I take from now on in regard to priest sexual abuse will be to show compassion for survivors and to make every human effort to prevent any child sexual abuse in the future.

The Pope can also advise cardinals, archbishops, bishops, and other priests who have been involved in protecting the Church and showing disregard for children to make similar public statements of accountability.

In addition, the Pope can institute policies where priests who have abused children in the past and any who are discovered to have sexually abused children to make full confessions on the steps of St. Peter's. This is an example of what these priests can say.

> I was selfish and insensitive. I took advantage of my position as a priest. The children believed I was special. They believed I was God's representative on earth. The children were afraid to say no to me. I hurt them. I am sorry. I will do whatever I have to do to make sure I do not hurt any other children again. I abused my power. I knew deep down I had power over children and they would do what I wanted.

> I did not care what the children wanted. I wanted the incredible pleasure I got from sexually abusing children. What children wanted and needed from me did not matter. All that mattered was what I wanted. I fooled myself into believing the children enjoyed the sex, but in my heart I knew better. The children wanted me to love then, but not in sexual ways. Children required my fond regard and guidance and not exploitation. Whatever abuse I experienced in the past is not excuse for my own abuse.

> I betrayed my priestly vows. I am sorry. I will do whatever it takes to make up for the hurt I have caused. By my acts of sexual abuse, I have shown callous disregard for the welfare of children.

A Fairy Tale?

Are public statements of wrong-doings a fairy tale? A fantasy? Do the Pope, others responsible for not protecting children, and abusing priest truly believe Church doctrine? If they do, they will make full public confessions that are broadcast throughout the world. Showing how to be accountable can have an enormous impact for good.

Personal Note

Dare we hope that it's over? The refusal of Church officials to protect children and hold priest perpetrators accountable are sins and crimes of high magnitude. As a Catholic, I am heartbroken and angry for many reasons. I think about the guilt I have felt my whole life for my unkind deeds--which can't hold a candle to what priests, bishops, archbishops, cardinals, and popes have done to harm others. Shame on them. Tragic for Catholics. Tragic for me who wants a spiritual home.

I don't believe it will be over until the Pope and everyone else involved in past cover-ups make full public confessions and then show their repentance through vigorous protection of children from predatory priests.

References

Allen, John. L. (2010). A papal conversion. *New York Times,* Sunday, March 28, p. 11.

Gilgun, Jane (2010). *Child Sexual Abuse: From Harsh Realities to Hope.* Amazon.

Gilgun, Jane. (2010). What child sexual abuse means to survivors.

Gilgun, Jane. (2010). What child sexual abuse means to abusers.

Gilgun, Jane. (2010). What child sexual abuse means to girl and women survivors.

Gilgun, Jane (2010). Coping with the effects of child sexual abuse.

Goodstein, Laurie & David Callender (2010). For half a century, deaf boys raised alarm on priest's abuse. *The New York Times*, Saturday, March 27, 2010, pp. A1, A10.

9

The Sex Education of Children

A good sex education is a life-long gift

Review: *"My grandson is really enjoying his Kindle....just a written essay of author's opinion. You got your dollar. That was your purpose."*

A good sex education is a life-long gift that parents can give their children. Talking to children about sexuality opens many channels of communication besides sexuality. Talking about sex as a natural part of life and signals to children that their parents are emotionally available and sensitive to them. If parents do not talk about sex with their children, children are left on their own to interpret the confusing and often destructive messages that they get from peers, the mass media, and the internet. These sources of information are distorted and may even be frightening and dangerous.

If children do not learn otherwise, they may act in ways that hurt themselves and others. It is up to parents to provide children with information that helps children make good decisions about their own sexual behaviors.

When parents do not talk to their children about sexuality, children are unlikely to talk to parents. Studies show that children who have received a good sex education tell parents if someone has touched them inappropriately, except if abusers have scared these children into silence. Studies also show that young people who have received a good sex education delay sexual intercourse by an average of three years.

Children of such parents therefore not only have good information about sexuality but they have secure attachments to their parents. From secure attachments, they have learned to "sniff out" people who want to use them sexually and naturally gravitate toward people who are as respectful as they have learned to be. Of course, some people are brilliant manipulators and can fool even the most securely attached and well-adjusted young people.

Start Early

Sex education starts in infancy. For example, when parents teach infants and toddlers the names of various body parts such as nose, eyes, and knees, they can teach them correct terms for their sexual body parts that are between the collarbone and knees, such as vagina, vulva, penis, anus, buttocks, and breasts. It is okay to also use "pet" and family names for sexual body parts, but knowledge of the more formal terms is important, too.

Pet names are part of family customs and build intimacy. These names also normalize sexual body parts. However, when children go to the doctor or if they have problems with others about sexuality, it is important that they can use terms that others understand. In situations where children are sexually abused or sexually harassed, those who have had a good sex education are more likely to communicate clearly and without shame that someone has violated them sexually.

Simple Explanations

As children become preschool age, they have questions about where babies come from. They also notice that boys and girls have different sexual organs. They are intrigued. Simple explanations satisfy children. "Girls have vulvas and vaginas. Boys have penises and testicles. When girls get older, they will have breasts like Mommy's. When boys get older, their breasts will be like Daddy's." That's pretty much all parents need to say.

Children learn from pictures. There are many excellent books that show the human body. Children are curious and not shocked by anatomically correct pictures. Parents who think children will be embarrassed often are surprised when they show relaxed curiosity and not shock and embarrassment.

Sexual Touching

Infants, toddlers, and preschool children often touch their sexual body parts and may touch the sexual body parts of other children. This gives parents opportunities to teach children about public and private sexual behaviors and appropriate and inappropriate sexual behaviors. They can find age-appropriate books and videos, use them with the children, and talk about sexuality.

Often this requires just a few minutes, and the children are ready to do something else. Masturbation is an important topic. Parents can instruct children that it is okay to masturbate, but that is a private activity not done in front of others. The places to masturbate or touch their sexual body parts are the privacy of their bedrooms or in other private places.

Sexual Respect

Parents have the important task of teaching children to respect the personal space and the sexual body parts of others. A no touching rule can be taught. "Please do not touch other people without their consent." "Please do not touch other people on their sexual body parts." "Keep your hands to yourself." "If someone touches you after you tell the person to stop, please tell me." "If someone touches your sexual body parts, please tell me."

These are guidelines that parents can provide children that help ensure safety from inappropriate actions of others. Furthermore, the guidelines help children to become safe to be around because they have learned to be appropriate with others.

Sophisticated Information

As children become older, the kinds of information they require gets more sophisticated, such as what kinds of behaviors are appropriate at what ages. For example, when is kissing okay? Necking? Petting? When is it appropriate to have sexual intercourse? How can you tell if he or she loves you? What do you do if someone pressures you to have sex? What if you like that person or think you are in love? What is sexual assault? What is rape? Is pressuring someone to have sexual contact a form of rape? Answer: yes. These are difficult topics to broach with children and teens.

A clear rule to teach older children is "No one can touch you without your consent. This includes sexual touching."

From exposure to messages from the mass media, young people may believe in "instant intimacy" where, soon after meeting, the dashing young man and the alluring young woman fall into each other's arms, make tender love, and are together forever. Girls may not know that boys are taught to be conquerors and may not love them at all, while girls believe sex means love.

Parents can compete with these distorted messages by through the example of their own domestic relationships and by talking to children about the various reasons that people are sexual with each other.

These reasons include one night stands for a bit of fun, to prove sexual prowess, convenience, to maintain a steady source of sex without love or commitment, friends with privileges, and sex as an expression of positive regard, love, and commitment. Parents can help children work out which kind of relationship the potential sexual partner seeks and whether

81

there is a match between what both persons want. In some situations, sex means very little but a chance to get your "rocks" off.

It is important for young people to know at what points in relationships various expressions of affection are appropriate. For example, some young people let themselves be pressured into sex by people for whom they do not have a secure relationship of trust. Yielding to pressure does not provide a foundation for a meaningful connection. Others are so overcome with powerful emotions that they have consensual sex with people they do not know well.

In these situations, some young people may think having sex means they now have a relationship of trust, affection, and love. The people they have had sex with, however, may not see things this way, but see themselves as getting lucky or having one more sexual encounter to brag about to their friends.

Parents have a responsibility to help children understand the various reasons people have for engaging in sexual touching, oral sex, and sexual intercourse. The goal is to help children develop into responsible and responsive human beings who celebrate their sexuality but who also do not exploit others and others do not exploit them. What's more, celebrating their sexuality means they know the difference between casual sex, exploitive sex, sexual assault, sex as affection, and sex as part of trust, love, and long-term commitment. Children do not learn this from the internet or from peers.

Children need long-term guidance to learn how not to exploit others sexually or not to harass or abuse. Direct instruction about these matters is the responsibility of parents. Parents may not be prepared to do this well. They must make an effort through reading and parent training to learn how to help their children understand the many complications that can arise in their sexual lives.

No Excuses

Children appreciate parents' efforts. Embarrassment is no excuse for parents not to educate children sexually. Out of embarrassment, some parents avoid and dismiss children's concerns and questions. That hurts children's developing sexuality and could lead to cut-offs in parent-child communication if children are sexually abused or have sex-related issues that require adult attention.

Excellent Resources

There are many excellent resources for parents. Jan Hindman's *A Very Touching Book* is humorous and informative. Young children, school-age children, and teenagers enjoy this book and learn from it. Chose books like Jan's—simple, direct, and with a touch of lightness. It is important to choose books that are appropriate to children's developmental level.

The Sex Information and Education Council of the United States has excellent information, as does StopItNow! and the Skillman Center for Children, located in Detroit, Michigan, USA. Parents have a responsibility to educate themselves so that they can educate their children.

Summary

Direct, accurate, and loving instruction about sexuality contributes to children's happiness and well-being and enhances parent-child relationships. Sexuality is not isolated from the rest of life. Other aspects of human functioning, such as self-respect, respect for others, and understanding the give and take in human relationships contribute to healthy sexuality. It is important for parents to create a harmonious family life where respect and give and take are the norm.

Fostering children's healthy sexual development is a life-long gift that parents can give their children. It takes time and effort. Parents have to deal with their own embarrassment. The price for avoiding sexual topics is high. Children are left on their own to interpret the confusing and often destructive messages that they get from peers, the mass media, and the internet.

Note: This article is a chapter from the book *Child Sexual Abuse: From Harsh Realities to Hope,* available on Amazon, iBooks, Barnes & Noble, & Kobo.

10

The Thin Blue Line
of Police Brutality & Other Essays on Violence

Reviewer: *"Absolute crap….poorly written"*

In February 2009, a video camera mounted in a police car recorded several Minneapolis cops beating and kicking a man who was handcuffed and on the ground. Later, one of the cops texted, "It was a good fight."

That quote sums up what most forms of violence mean to perpetrators: Fun. Cops who behave in violent ways are no different from the men in prison I interviewed for a research project on violence. These convicted felons told me they use violence as a high, to feel the rush, to redress a wrong, to earn or keep respect, to restore honor, and to be part of a group.

Violent people believe victims deserve it. They decide who their victims are, and they act on their beliefs. A man beats a woman because women are supposed to respect men, and, according to him, she did not. A cop brutalizes a black man because according to him black men are dangerous. And they enjoy themselves.

At the time cops—and anyone else—commit violence, they are acting on deeply held beliefs. In their rational moments, they may know these beliefs are false stereotypes. The rush to violence is so powerful that cops—and anyone else—suspend their judgment and give in to the enjoyment of abusing their power over others. It's a rush, a badge of honor, fun. Their beliefs give them permission to indulge their violence. As one man said after a bar fight

> I've woken up in the morning with this lip hanging out here, eyes swollen shut, and my nose broken. I had my friends come over. We yucked it up. 'Ha, ha. That was a hell of a fight, wasn't it?' Somehow I was a man then.

Another man enjoyed instilling fear in others. He said

> My family's afraid. The people outside my family's afraid. Friends of my family's afraid. My sister's girlfriend, her and her

husband came over to the house one night. Her husband, like we got into an argument. I jumped up, and I grabbed him, slammed him up against the wall. Here's my sister crying. Here's this guy's wife—she's crying. I'm like, what are these people crying about? They're giving me this high, this, this feeling of control or power.

I got power now over these people. They're telling me, 'Oh don't hurt him. Don't hurt him.' My sister, she said, 'You don't know my brother. Control yourself. He might kill him.' I've got this power. I love that. I love people to dress me up.

To stop violence, we have to understand it. Violence is enjoyable and gratifying. Beliefs about victims justify violent acts.

The cops who are violent may not be much different from most other people. Violence is rooted deep in our hearts and brains. When we feel wronged or disrespected, few people do not think violent thoughts. When we are in situations where we think we can get away with violence with no consequences to ourselves, who is not tempted to experience the deep satisfaction of making others pay, teaching them a lesson, punishing them for some wrong that we perceive?

Ordinary people have something in common with rapists, murderers, and child molesters—and brutal cops. We think violent thoughts and may do violent things when we think we can get away with them. We commit everyday acts of violence, such as blaming others for our mistakes.

I am not saying that everyday acts of violence have the devastating effects of rape, murder, child molestation, and police brutality. I am saying that our everyday acts often hurt other people and in the long run contribute to conditions that make egregious acts of violence possible. We human beings do not want to give up the comfort and satisfaction that comes from committing violence in our hearts.

Solzhenitsyn in *The Gulag Archipelago* recognized something similar when he wrote "… the line dividing good and evil cuts through the heart of every human being. And who is willing to destroy a part of his own heart?" Until we face up to the satisfaction we find in the violence we commit in our own hearts, we will not do what it takes to prevent violence that does deep and long-lasting harm to victims and those who love them.

Cops who commit brutal acts, convicted felons, and those who get away with violence are human beings. What we have in common with them is the violence in our own hearts and minds that permits violence to continue. Why stop? I enjoy it. Those are the words of a convicted violent felon. Those words fit a lot of us.

There is a thin blue line between police brutality and the brutality of convicted felons. There is another thin blue line between the rest of us and convicted felons.

Note:

In February 2009, a Minneapolis cop stopped Derrick Jenkins for speeding in a 30 mile per hour zone. The cop wrestled Jenkins to the ground. Several other cops showed up. The beat and kicked Jenkins while he was on the ground. A video camera in the squad car recorded the incident. The cops' report stated that Jenkins had resisted arrest and that they had used necessary force to subdue him.

Jenkins lost his license and was charged with resisting arrest and assaulting a police officer. The video contradicted the report. Police supervisors reviewed the video and concluded that the cops had done nothing wrong, but they did recommend that all charges be dropped, which they were. Jenkins was shamed and humiliated and did not protest what the cops had done to him. He just wanted it all to go away.

When a cop arrested Harvard scholar Henry Louis Gates in his own home in July of 2009, Jenkins decided to speak out. The FBI is now investigating the Jenkins case. Jenkins is considering a lawsuit. Like Professor Gates, he wants to bring race-based matters out into the public forum for discussion. The video is widely available on the internet.

Note: This is one of four essays in the four-essay collection.

11

Turtle Night at Playa Grande

Reviewer: *"check out a good sea turtle website instead"*

Late at night, a mother leatherback turtle arises from the Pacific Ocean at Playa Grande, a sandy beach in Costa Rica, Central America. She is as big as oil barrel and weighs as much as a horse. White dots speckle her body. Five bony ridges go from the top of her head to her tail. Her back looks like a giant bike helmet. She has a hooked nose and her eyes bug out from the sides of her head.

She is a visitor from the distant past. For millions of years, since the time dinosaurs ruled the earth, leatherbacks have come ashore to lay their eggs. This mother used her long, wide flippers like wings to soar like a bird for thousands of miles from the ocean waters of Malaysia to reach Playa Grande, where she was born ten years before.

On the beach, the mother leatherback lifts her head and looks around her. Lights, sounds, and smells of predators would send her back to the sea. The beach is dark and still. Nothing moves except the waves of the ocean. The salt water scents the air.

She plows slowly forward using her front and back flippers. Her breath comes in gasps and sighs. Tears stream from her eyes. No one knows why she cries. Maybe it's from the hard work of moving across the sand. Maybe she's washing the sea salt from her eyes.

She leaves behind four-foot wide tracks. The tracks look like a bulldozer had come through. When she is away from the reach of the waves, she sweeps aside the sand with her front flippers until she has made a shallow pit. She pushes herself into the pit and raises her left back flipper. She waits a few seconds. Then she slowly scoops out about a cup of sand and flicks it to the side. She waits a few more seconds. She lowers her back right flipper into the hole she has made. She pulls out another cup of sand and flicks it away.

Over and over, she raises and lowers her back flippers one at a time until she has dug a deep, narrow hole. Then she rests.

When she is ready, she stands over the hole and a white egg a little bigger than a golf ball drops into the hole. It's leathery and bounces a bit but does not break. She rests again. Another egg drops and then another. Soon there are more than 80 eggs in the hole. Some mothers lay more than 100 eggs. Others lay about 40. In one season, leatherbacks lay eggs from three to eleven times. With her right front flipper, she pats the eggs. She slowly pushes the sand back into the hole with her flippers. When the hole is almost full, she pats the sand.

Then she dances. She swings her right front flipper forward and churns up the sand. She swings her left front flipper forward and churns up the sand. She takes a step back and churns up more sand. She moves sideways and then toward the front, churning all the time. When she's done, the sand looks like a battleground. Predators will not know where her eggs are.

It's almost dawn. The humid air of Playa Grande had made her warm. She has to get back to the ocean to cool off. If she overheats, she will die. She pushes herself toward the ocean. She doesn't look back.

For long sunny days, the eggs incubate under the sand. Inside, baby turtles grow. In about two months, toward the end of a hot, humid day, a tiny black nose pokes out of the sand. Then another and another.

Soon the beach is alive with baby leatherbacks. They fit in the palm of a child's hand and look like wind-up toys. They have lines of white dots down the ridges of their backs.

Their flippers are outlined in white, too. With their flippers, they push themselves toward the sea. They move slowly, a little bit at a time.

A lone gull drops from the sky. She screeches with open mouth and grabs one of the baby leatherbacks. Off she flies with the baby in her mouth. Her screeches attract a second gull that dives to snatch another baby and soar away.

The remaining babies push on. A wave washes over them and rolls back to the sea. The babies tumble on their backs. Their flippers pump against the air. They turn on their sides and push themselves upright. They follow the water that slides into the sea.

Finally, the baby leatherbacks reach the place where the shore meets the sea. They slip into the water and disappear. The male leatherbacks will never again return to land. They spend their lives in oceans and seas.

When the females are about ten years old, they will return to Playa Grande late at night. Like their mother before them and all the other mothers back to the time of dinosaurs, these mother leatherbacks will soar like birds through thousands of miles of ocean to reach the land where they were born. There, they will dig nests and lay their own eggs. A few babies will reach adulthood, and the cycle of life will continue.

More About Leatherback Turtles,
the Giants of the Sea

Leatherbacks are the biggest of ocean turtles and among the largest living reptiles. Adults are from 5 to 10 feet long and weigh from 600 to 2000 pounds. They are longer than many cars. Small leatherbacks weigh as much as ponies and large ones more than Budweiser draft horses. People look like matchsticks when they stand beside the giant leatherbacks.

With their bony ridges, hooked nose, and huge barrel-shaped bodies, it is easy to understand why people centuries ago thought leatherbacks were sea monsters.

Leatherbacks are one of seven kinds of sea turtles. Other sea turtles are much smaller. Loggerhead turtles and green sea turtles, for example, are about three feet long and weigh 150 to 400 pounds.

The smaller turtles can be seen in many aquariums in the United States and in other countries. Leatherbacks cannot live in captivity. They continually bump against the walls of aquariums until they die.

Like other reptiles, such as dinosaurs, alligators, and snakes, leatherbacks are cold-blooded. Reptiles have body temperatures that match the air or water around them. When the environment is cold, most reptiles become sluggish or even inactive.

Leatherbacks are different. Oily tissue under their leathery shells insulates them against cold water. Human beings would quickly die in waters that are home to leatherbacks.

Their layer of oily tissue permits them to live throughout the oceans of the world. They are found in the warm waters off the coasts of Asia, Central America, South America, and the United States. People have spotted leatherbacks in the frigid north Atlantic and north Pacific Oceans. They even go into the water of the Arctic Circle.

In the tropics, where mother leatherbacks lay their eggs, it's very hot. If leatherbacks stay on land too long, they can overheat and die. As soon as they finish laying their eggs, they get back to the cool ocean waters as fast as they can. Maybe that's why they don't look back after they dance over their nesting sites.

When they are active, leatherbacks swim to the surface every few minutes to breathe. At rest, they stay underwater for an hour or more. They have been known to dive more than 4000 feet.

Their diet is mostly jellyfish. Like the leatherbacks themselves, the ancestors of jellyfish lived in oceans when dinosaurs roamed the earth.

Leatherbacks have had a good supply of food for millions of years. Inside their mouths and down their throats are spines that snare jellyfish and other soft sea creatures of the sea.

A mother leatherback comes to shore three or more times to lay her eggs. That means she produces hundreds of eggs in one season. In her trip to shore, a mother sometimes digs three or four holes for nests only to have the sides collapse. The sand has to have just the right amount of moisture for the walls to hold.

Leatherbacks wait until high tide to build their nests. High tide is when the waves of the ocean reach furthest up the beaches. The nests are above the high water mark. This protects the eggs from being pulled into the water going back to the sea.

Whether the eggs hatch into males or females depends upon the air and sand temperature. When the temperature is warm, more females emerge from the eggs. If the temperature lowers even a few degrees, more males are born.

Newly hatched turtle babies are attracted to light. In the dark of night, the horizon over the ocean is the brightest area the babies see. They push themselves toward this light. During egg-laying season on beaches that are inhabited, many people turn off their lights at night so the baby turtles won't move toward light that is away from the shore. When babies do this, they die.

Lights created by people are only one of many threats to leatherbacks. Seabirds, people, and land animals eat the eggs. For every thousand babies hatched, only a few live to adulthood. Sea birds, sharks, and other fish eat most of the babies. The leatherbacks that survive to adulthood are threatened by human predators, ocean pollution, and fishing nets.

People kill adult leatherbacks for their oily tissue. Oil is squeezed from the tissue and is prized for waterproofing boats and for oil lamps. Some people hunt leatherbacks for their meat.

Balloons, plastic bags and cups are found in the stomachs of dead leatherbacks that wash ashore. The turtles mistake these objects for jellyfish. Clear plastic bags especially look like jellyfish. The plastic kills them. Pollution from oil spills often suffocates leatherbacks.

Hundreds of leatherbacks are caught each year in giant fishing nets that hold them underwater. They can't get to the surface to breathe, and they drown. Dolphins, too, are killed by these nets that can be up to seventy miles long. Countries throughout the world have passed laws so that fishnets have escape holes for turtles, dolphins, and other large sea creatures. Fewer leatherbacks drown in nets than in the past.

People build houses and hotels on beaches where mother

leatherbacks make their nests. Mother leatherbacks will return to the sea without nesting if they hear noise, see lights, or smell animals or people who hunt and eat the eggs. Beaches are sometimes washed away when people build on them.

Some ocean shores in Central and South America and Asia have serious problems with erosion and increased human populations. On those beaches, the number of nesting sites has gone down. Other less inhabited shores have seen a great increase of leatherback nesting sites. This is the exception to the rule that female leatherbacks return to beaches where they were hatched.

We have more to learn about leatherbacks. For example, no one knows how long they live. How the females find their way back to the places where they were born is another mystery. Scientists think they may follow the earth's magnetic fields. They also could be guided by sight, taste, and smell.

How often they lay their eggs also is not known for sure. Some people think it's every other year or two, while others say it's every three or four years. Even why they cry when they're on land is something else no one knows about the mysterious leatherbacks.

Leatherback turtles swam the oceans when dinosaurs ruled the earth. Dinosaurs are extinct. That means they will never again roam the earth. People of all ages can help make sure that leatherbacks do not become extinct. Recycling plastic, putting trash in barrels and not throwing it into oceans, and supporting laws that protect leatherbacks will ensure that leatherbacks survive millions years into the future.

If you want to know more

Leatherbacks cannot live in aquariums. The only way to see them is to go to their nesting sites on a guided turtle watch. The tours are strictly regulated by local police. Be prepared to see very big turtles and to stay up late at night.

EARTHWATCH has news bout leatherback turtles. http://www.earthwatch.org/europe/newsroom/science/news-3-leatherbackcomeback.

Volunteers work with scientists to help at the leatherback egg hatchery, to develop new hatching grounds as older ones disappear, and to learn more about the mysterious leatherbacks. When the females come to shore, they are tagged with a radio transmitter. This way, the turtles can be tracked as they swim the world's oceans.

The National Geographic society has information about leatherbacks.

http://animals.nationalgeographic.com/animals/reptiles/leatherback-sea-turtle/

The Vancouver Aquarium has an informative website about leatherbacks. http://www.vanaqua.org/learn/aquafacts/reptiles/leatherback-turtles.

Turtle Trax has a website on sea turtles. At this site, you'll see pictures and drawings of sea turtles, hear their sounds, and read stories about them. This address is http://www.turtles.org/

12

What Sexual Abuse Means
to Child Survivors

Children think sexual abuse is their fault

Children have a lot to say about their own sexual abuse. Their stories show that they are aware of the power that adults have over them, and they are afraid to resist. They are taught to obey adults or older people, especially people with authority, such as parents, grandparents, teachers, babysitters, and social service professionals. They dread consequences if they refuse to obey. Children often think that sexual abuse is their fault. They think they were supposed to have been able to stop the abuse. Unfortunately, many people blame children, too.

Children often know little about specific sexual behaviors and may lack the vocabulary to talk about sexual abuse, but they understand taboos and shame associated with sexual abuse and sexuality. Many understand the consequences for themselves and for their families if they tell others that they have been sexually abused. In some cases, their fears are unfounded, but in many others, they have reason to be afraid.

This chapter may be hard to read. However, it shows the harsh realities that survivors experience. Grappling with harsh realities leads to hope and recovery. For adults to be sensitively responsive to survivors of child sexual abuse, they too must grapple with the harsh realities. Otherwise, they will distance themselves from children and other survivors. Recovery is possible through emotional connection with trusted others who are psychologically available, attuned, and empathic.

Children Believe They Must Obey

Children think they have to obey persons in authority. Randy, ten, was sexually abused by a teenage boy named Hank who was her babysitter. She thought she had to do what he said. He told her, "Go to the bathroom." She said, "I went to the bathroom." He jumped out from behind a shower curtain, pulled her off the toilet, placed her on the floor, and sexually abused her.

Olivia, eleven, abused between the ages of five and eight by a man who was a father figure to her mother and a grandfather figure to her said

I thought there were laws about adults and children.

Lisa, nine, abused from the age of three to age nine, said of the abuser who was her grandfather

He was big. I was little. I had to do what he said.

Vickie, seven, refused to go home for supper when her brother and sister went to get her in the park. She told them, "I'm waiting for someone." She was waiting for the man who had sexually abused her earlier that day. She said

I waited because he told me to. I listened. I was small.

Children Think Sexual Abuse is Their Fault

Many child survivors blame themselves for the abuse, even when they recognize that the perpetrators forced them. Lisa, nine, said

My grandfather forced me. He unzipped his pants. He put his hand on mine and put my hand on his penis. He held my hand there until he was done. I took my hand off when he let go of me.

The abuse took place on a boat. Lisa said

I felt like jumping off the boat and swimming to shore, but I can't swim.

Despite Lisa's recognition of being forced, she said

It was my fault. I didn't tell him not to do it.

Randy, the girl who was assaulted in the bathroom, said the abuse was "sort of" her fault "because I went into the bathroom and was sitting on the toilet." Randy could not put the pieces of her experience together. She went into the bathroom because Hank had told her to, but she could not see that the assault and the directive to go into the bathroom make the abuse his responsibility and not hers.

Donna, fifteen, assaulted by her brother, sexually abused by her grandfather, and the victim of an attempted rape by her best friend's father, thought she must be at fault. She said, "My judgment must be impaired." She was confused, hurt, and ashamed that three different males abused her sexually. The "guy" was her best friend's father. He was driving them home from choir practice.

Some Adults Blame Children

Children blame themselves because so many adults blame them.

For example, in the case of Donna, a county attorney who prosecuted the case against her best friend's father, said to her in her mother's presence

> Why didn't you get out of the car when that guy went after you? I think you really wanted it.

Carla ran away from home because she felt blamed for the incest her father committed. She said

> My father was bitching. I asked my mother what he was bitching about. She said, 'He said it was all your fault. I'm breaking up the family.' I couldn't take it. I took off.

Carla was thirteen and lived on the streets for six months.

Not all children think sexual abuse is their fault, but it is a common belief. Caring adults can gently ask children, "Do you think you did something wrong?" or "Sometimes kids think the abuse is their fault. Do you?" It is surprising how eagerly some children answer questions like these. Their answers also can be surprising, such as Lisa's when she said it was her fault because she never told her grandfather not to do it.

It is important for adults to give children opportunities to talk about whether they are at fault. It is also important for children to be able to express themselves in their own ways. Adults, maybe because of their own anxieties, want to reassure children by saying, "It's not your fault." Of course it is not children's fault, but if they believe it is, such a statement can invalidate their experience. The timing of "It's not your fault" can make a difference in children's recovery. It's more helpful to ask children why they think it's their fault and allow a conversation to unfold.

Girls and boys whose mothers sexually abused them may prefer to think that they did something wrong rather than to think that their mothers did. They often struggle with disbelief and self-blame.

Self-Blame Wide-Spread

Children are not alone in blaming themselves for the harm that others do to them. Adult survivors of rape and women in physically violent and emotionally abusive relationship believe abuse is their fault, too. Men who experience their wives and partners as verbally, physically, and sexually abusive often think they did something to cause these behaviors. Individuals are not to blame for their own abuse. The only persons who are responsible are abusers.

Children's Understandings

Younger children often do not understand sexual behaviors. Randy, who went into the bathroom after her babysitter told her to, described what the teenager did

> He pulled me off the toilet seat, and he dripped something. I was on the ground of the bathroom, and he sort of did pushups on me.

Lisa, abused for six years, said, "Grandpa used to do it on the boat until stuff came out. He had sort of a grin on his face." Nan, eleven, said, "I never heard of any of the things he did like that." Olivia said

> It's hard, what he did to me. I couldn't stand to do it to anybody. All the germs and stuff you get.

Older children may not understand sexual behaviors, either. Emily, thirteen, said she thought her great uncle was trying to love her. When asked when she thought of that, she said

> It felt kind of weird. I didn't like him the way I liked boys.

Carla, also thirteen, said about a conversation she had with a girlfriend

> We were just talking one day. She was talking about her boyfriend. She thought she was big. She had sex with a seventeen year-old. I said to her, 'That's nothing. I go to bed with a thirty-four year-old.' She said, 'You do? Who is he?' I said, 'My father.' 'You don't do that,' she said.

When her girlfriend told her that her father is not supposed to do that, the girlfriend struck a chord. Carla knew immediately that her girlfriend was right. She was ashamed.

Ursula, fourteen, molested since she was seven and sexualized as a result, said

> My father never explained sex to me. I had to learn by myself. I learned on the street. My father told me last year. Too late.

Her father was worried because Ursula walked the streets at night looking for men to have sex with. He was a single parent. African-American, he sought help, but he found the professionals and clergy he consulted to be unhelpful. This parent had reason to be worried. The police found Ursula's body in an alley when she was sixteen years old. She had been raped and murdered.

Children's Understanding of Abuse

Many children do not know what sexual abuse is. Katie, thirteen, said

> I didn't know grown-ups did it to kids.

Olivia said about a fourteen year-old boy who molested her

My mother never told me about molestation. I was confused when he did it. He should have been more mature.

Even when parents warn their children about family members who sexually abuse children, they may not understand. Emily said about her great uncle who sexually abused her

My mother told me something about him. I didn't know what he did to me was the same thing.

Children require explicit information. This is an example of what to say: "Your uncle touches children on their breasts, buttocks, vulvas, vaginas, and penises. If he touches you there, I want you to tell me right way, no matter what he says. Don't listen to anything he says. He may say he will get in trouble, or you will break up the family, or you will get in trouble, or he will kill you. Pretend you believe him, and then tell me. I will take care of it."

Sometimes children learn about molestation by strangers but do not know that people they know abuse children sexually. Nan, eleven, was molested by her babysitter when she was eight. She had no idea that people she knew could sexually abuse her. She said

My mother never told me about this. She told me about strangers. She called it 'stranger danger.'

School programs that inform children about sexual abuse often are helpful, but not always. Vickie, ten, was molested by a stranger when she was six. She said about a police-sponsored prevention program featuring Office Friendly

Officer Friendly came too late. If he would've come sooner, this wouldn't have happened.

Vickie said that when the molester pressed his penis against her she went "blank." She continued

I didn't think of anything. I was wondering. just regular wondering what it meant. What he was doing and stuff. I wondered what was going to happen.

Older children may not understand child sexual abuse, either. Carla believed her father when he told her that what they are doing is what all fathers and daughters do. She said

I loved my father. I still do, but he still ruined my life. He should have told me what we were doing was wrong.

Education about sexuality sometimes is less complete than parents think it is. Donna said about being victimized by three different males

My mother always told me that sex with love was beautiful. I didn't love those men, so what I did was dirty and awful.

Sexual Sensations

Children may experience sexual sensations. As mentioned, earlier, Olivia said

Sometimes it felt good, but that made me feel guilty. Sometimes it stung. Why is that?

Pat, a woman survivor, said about the sexual abuse her father perpetrated

When I was real, real young, he would put his penis between my legs. And I would come. I mean I would feel pleasure. I don't know it would be come back then. Do you know what I'm saying?

Some children take pleasure in the attention but the sexual contact is confusing and unwanted. Andy said of his uncle

I felt like he cared for me, and that was pleasurable to me. I don't think specifically the sexual act was that pleasurable for me because it was more uncomfortable. I was scared, but I know it was probably the first time I felt there was an adult who really cared for me, and that made me feel good. That was pleasurable. So it may be that I wanted to--maybe not sought out, but enjoyed the time with him, but not specifically the sexual acts, but just feeling cared for by an adult. I think I liked that.

He continued

I never thought my parents did [love me], and in some ways today, I still don't believe that my parents love me. He was the first person who, like, spent time with me and did things with me, made me feel like I was okay. That confuses things there and makes it worse, because I was scared. Then I felt cared for. I was confused, and yet he made me feel better.

Andy summed up a lot about how children understand sexuality and sexual abuse. He said

I mean in society it's such a taboo thing, sexuality as a whole when you're a small child. You don't learn about that. You don't know about it. You just know that it's wrong because you don't pull down your pants for someone, because you don't expose your genitals. You know that that's all wrong just from growing up.

Some people think the children wanted the abuse if they seem to have experienced sexual sensations, or if there was orgasm and/or ejaculation involved. In actuality, human beings, including young children, respond to sexual stimulation, which is pleasurable to the body but not necessarily to the mind. Children may feel dirty and ashamed about any bodily responses. They do not want or understand the sexual acts, but their bodies may respond. Physical pleasure from sexual abuse is confusing to children.

Many adults are unprepared to deal with the reality that children may feel sexual sensations while they are being sexually abused and that this may be confusing and shameful to them. This simply is too hard for many adults to handle, and so they avoid the topic. They do not follow up or inquire about any possible sensations and confusion about sensations the children may want to discuss. Children thus are left without adult guidance and understanding, which is neglect of children's emotional and psychological well-being.

Vivid Descriptions

Children can provide vivid descriptions of perpetrators and what happens during abusive acts. These descriptions bring to life the power differences between adults and children. Each incident is unique. In their own words, children show how little and powerless they felt when in the presence of adults and older people who wanted to sexually abuse them. They felt compelled to obey and were fearful of consequences if they did not. In some of their descriptions, however, children show how they resisted the power abusers had over them.

Randy, ten at the time of the abuse, said she could never forget what Hank, the teenage perpetrator, looked like because

I was scared. That guy was really tall. He was scary looking.

Hank assaulted Randy twice. She said

The first day he did the thing in the bathroom with me, and the second day he pulled down my pants and kissed me on the fanny. He's really sick.

She described how he got her into the bathroom.

He had this puppet. He had it say, 'Go into the bathroom.' So I did. I don't know how he got there before me.

Hank had hidden behind the shower curtain. When he stepped out from behind it, Randy said

I almost had a heart attack. I was sitting on the toilet.

Hank made no attempt to persuade Randy to cooperate. As he stepped from behind the shower curtain, he said, "Shhh. Don't say anything." Then, as described earlier, he sexually assaulted her. Randy said "he dripped something" out of his penis. She also said she only had her shirt on. Randy protested:

> I asked him what he was doing. I said, 'Get out of here.' He said, 'Don't you dare scream.'

She had no idea what he was doing. Randy told her mother right away. The mother phoned the police, and the boy was charged with sexual assault and court-ordered into adolescent sex offender treatment.

Randy still saw Hank because he lived in the neighborhood. She described him. Her revulsion is evident.

> I mean, he's a super gross-out. He has long hair and sort of a beard, too, like an ape. He doesn't have any class or anything. He looks like he probably drools all the time. He's a gag. He's a gross barf-out.

Randy was unable to explain why she went into the bathroom when he told her to. When asked if she would have obeyed a six year-who told her to go into the bathroom, she said, "No," as if the answer were self-evident. Randy was in the gifted program at school. Randy resisted and told her mother after the second, but not the first incident.

Olivia, also in a gifted school program, is the child who thought there were laws about adults and children that children had to obey. She said that meant

> Someone older than me I had to obey them.

She had several other reasons why she did not actively resist and tell her mother. Some of these reasons were mentioned earlier. The prime reason was the abuser's manipulation of her concern for the well being of others. The abuser told her that if she told anyone he would have to go to jail and that would make his wife unhappy. He asked her

> You don't want to make my wife unhappy, do you?

Olivia gave other reasons that had to do with fear, self-sacrifice, and confusion.

> I was scared. I didn't know what to do. He was doing this, and I didn't want him to do it. At that stage, I didn't say 'no' to people. I always knew there was somebody who was worse off than I was. He played on that.

He also told her

'Doing this make me feel good. You like to make people feel good, don't you?'

She did, of course, but not through being forced to touch his genitals or submitting to his invasive touch. Olivia was afraid of what he would do if she resisted, even though she believed he liked her. This is what she said.

> He did like me. He was probably senile. I did what he wanted. I felt he would do something to me. I didn't know why. I didn't know what. I guess I didn't understand.

If fact, she understood exactly what the man wanted her to understand. The sexual abuse consisted of masturbation and oral sex.

> I used to rub his penis outside his pants. I did it right on his front porch. Sometimes he put his hands in my pants and rubbed me. He made me put his penis in my mouth. He did it a lot of times. I didn't like that.

Olivia thought her mother used to see her with the man on his front porch, "but my mother never said anything to me." She was too young and too naïve to know what their behaviors meant, except that she did not like them. For two and a half years, whenever this man called her over, she went. One day, she was playing with a girlfriend. When the man called her over, she and her girlfriend went. The man took the two girls into his living room. Olivia said

> He had us sit down, and he put his hands in my pants. He said to my friend, 'Come on over. It feels nice.' My friend ran out the door.

Later, she talked to her friend about the incident.

> I said I was sorry. I knew what was going to happen, and it did. I was scared to say anything to her.

Seeing her friend run away and the man did nothing gave her ideas of what to do the next time he tried to touch her.

> I cried and told him I didn't want to do it. He didn't do it again.

Soon afterward, she and her family moved from the neighborhood. She visited the man and his wife several times with her mother. When the man died, she told her mother about the sexual abuse. She said

> I figured that he had died. He couldn't go to jail if I told. I wouldn't make his wife unhappy if I told my mother.

Her mother was deeply shocked. This man had been a father figure to her for ten years. She arranged for professional help for Olivia, for herself, and for the rest of the family.

Physical Violence

Many incidents of sexual abuse do not involve physical violence, but some do. For example, some children witness physical abuse of their mothers. When their fathers begin to touch them sexually, they are afraid to resist. Alberta was eleven when he father first sexually abused her. He told her to take her clothes off. She said

> I don't know why I just didn't leave. The idea didn't occur to me....My mother tried to stop him. She got between us. What could she do? He just pushed her away and beat her up.

Her father told her that what he was doing to her was "an everyday thing. People do it every day." He tried to have intercourse with her that first time. She said

> I felt sick to my stomach. I didn't want him to do it. I wanted him to stop. I hated it.

She did not tell him to stop because

> I would get hit with a belt. So I did what he said every time.

While he was abusing her,

> My father told me I was jealous of my mother. He said I wanted to have sex with him the way my mother did, but I wasn't jealous of that. I didn't even think of it.

Adults can be helpful to children who have been sexually abused if they understand that each child's experience is unique. Adults must, however, be ready for anything. What children say can be surprising and even shocking. The stories in this book can prepare adults to be open and receptive to whatever children have to say.

Discussion

Children have a lot to say about their own sexual abuse. They have surprising insights into what happened to them. Their accounts highlight how children perceive the power that adult and older abusers have over them. In their eyes, abusers are older, stronger, and have authority. They do strange and frightening things that children do not understand, but that children describe in vivid detail. Children feel the shame and blame of child sexual abuse and typically are confused.

Sensitive Responsiveness

Children who have been sexually abused require the sensitive, responsive, and wise attention of adults who listen, whose words are well-timed, who can soothe them, reassure them, and help them to understand that other people, even people they know and love, hurt them. Parents have to put aside their own outrage and hurt in order to be emotionally available to their children. Professionals can help parents through difficult times, but the support of family and friends is important, too.

Parents can expect that their own and their children's need for intense processing of the sexual abuse will diminish over time, but that children will periodically want to talk about their sexual abuse and so will parents. Parents must prepare themselves for on going processing of the meanings of the sexual abuse when their children want this.

Children and older survivors often benefit from professional help, such as individual therapy, family therapy, group therapy, and psychoeducation. Sensitive, responsive parents do whatever it takes to foster their children's healthy development.

It is the responsibility of perpetrators and anyone else who has hurt children to do major repair work. This includes taking responsibility for their behaviors and expressing their sadness, regrets for having hurt children, and taking actions that ensure they never again will sexually abuse or otherwise abuse their power.

Education About Sexual Abuse

Children require explicit education about sexual abuse. Vague statements do not help. Stating that child sexual abuse means touching children on their breasts, buttocks, penises, vulvas, and vaginas in secret protects children. Stating that sexualized talk or looks are unacceptable and they do not have to put up with it helps children. Telling children about the many kinds of threats that perpetrators may use protects children. Letting children know that fathers, mothers, sisters, brothers, aunts, uncles, grandfathers, grandmothers, social workers, teachers, coaches, and youth workers have been known to sexually abuse children protects children.

Children need to understand that any touch that is secret is a touch that parents want to know about. Children do not have to keep secrets when the secrets are about touching sexual body parts, or any other actions related to sexuality. Even if perpetrators make children promise not tell, children do not have to keep promises about secret sexual touches or anything else that hurts children and makes them feel bad.

Assuring children that parents will protect them helps children, but parents must be prepared to follow through on this promise, no matter the consequences. As one mother said, "I would rather live on the streets than allow someone to abuse my children." She in fact did lose her home and had to go to a shelter after she realized her husband was sexually abusing their toddler children. Within a few years, she had her own home again and supported her children financially. She had no regrets.

These are the harsh realities of child sexual abuse. Dealing directly with them leads to hope and a promising future.

Note: This article is a chapter from the book *Child Sexual Abuse: From Harsh Realities to Hope*, available on Amazon, iBooks, Barnes & Noble, Kobo, and other internet booksellers.

13

Why They Do It:
Beliefs & Emotional Gratification
Lead to Violent Acts

Reviewer: 1 *"A Speculative Rant--Not Objective Research"*
Reviewer 2: *"Not facts, all opinions"*
Reviewer 3:*" Very interesting....Wasn't quite what I expected"*

Mass murders of children in China and a local mass murder of adults in Minneapolis in April 2010 raise questions about why they do it. China and Minneapolis could hardly be more far apart, but the murderers in both countries have a lot in common. In this article, I will first present the general features of why people kill and do other violent things such as rape and physical violence. Then I will show how these general features can be used to understand individual cases.

People commit violent acts because of their beliefs. They also almost always get a strong emotional charge out of being violent. These two features are the core of why people are violent: Beliefs and emotional charge. There are many variations after that, but these are the constants. The examples of the exceptions that I know personally are cases where individuals stated they experienced no gratification for the murders they committed. In those cases, they felt they had to kill because someone had disrespected them, they wanted to control other people, and when they saw no way out but to participate in a gang killing. (These last two sentences I added after this article received the three one-star ratings.)

Beliefs

Violent people build an image of their victims in their minds. They decide who the victims are and then act on their beliefs. Who the victims think they are and who other people believe the victims are do not matter. All that matters is who perpetrators think their victims are.

Don

A graduate of an elite private college named Don decided the women he raped were "loose" and out looking for sex anyway so it was no big thing when he followed them home in the dark and raped them. This is the conversation I had with him when I interviewed him in a maximum security prison where he lived for 17 years.

> Um, and if I take the right person, you know, it's not going to make a difference anyway. You know, because, like I said before, you know, the women I was, was raping were, you know, they'd been in that bar looking for guys anyway....You know, all my victims were, you know, they, my set up was that they'd been out in bars or loose sexually, kinds of people. So they had it coming, or they, you know, it didn't matter to them. So, so, you know, this wouldn't be a big, big thing to happen to them.

After Don's statement that rape would not be "a big, big thing" to the women, I was speechless for 20 seconds. When I finally was able to speak, I asked Don how he knew the women were loose. His answer revealed more of his thinking:

> J: (10 sec) Yeah. (10 sec) Well, how did you know that they were at bars and were loose? What...[interrupted].

> D: Well, I mean, I didn't actually know that.

> J: Oh.

> D: I, I knew, I knew that because that's the kind of people that were out at that time of night.

> J: Okay. So you would be looking at what time of night?

> D: Yeah.

> J: What, what time of night would you be out?

> D: Well, generally the, and this, this is another thing that doesn't make sense because there was all kinds of times that I was out.

> J: Oh.

> D: But, generally it would be late, like you know, midnight, one o'clock, two o'clock in the morning, that kind of thing. But you know I was

out in, in the winter time sometimes after it got dark, you know, o not right after it got dark but maybe at seven-thirty or eight o'clock, or something.

Don decided that some women deserved to be raped and he acted on his beliefs. He was unable to step outside of his own frame of reference.

I saw this inability to step outside of a frame of reference repeatedly in research I did with about 100 men who had committed violent acts. Perpetrators are oblivious to the effects of their thinking and the actions that result from their thinking.

Harley

Don did not have personal relationships with the women he raped, but Harley only beat his wives and girlfriends. He beat them when he thought they disrespected them. Whether their actions showed disrespect is a matter of dispute. How he defined them and their behaviors is what lead to his actions. This is an example of Harley's beliefs.

> I brutally beat up one of my girlfriends one time because we had moved to this house. She had asked me to clean up the house. Vacuum the rugs is what it was because she wanted to put the furniture in, mop the floor. I went and got drunk. I came back. She asked me this at twelve o'clock. I came back in the house at nine-thirty. She had mopped the house and straightened the house up. The house looked good. I jumped on her and beat her up.
>
> In my mind, she was trying to make me look like an ass because she could have waited on me to clean up, to do this. She asked me to do it. I mean I just didn't only beat her up. I mean I knocked out all the windows in the house with my fist. I mean I'm standing here bleeding, my fingers, all these cuts and stuff like this on my hands. I'm standing there bleeding. She's bleeding. I mean I've beaten her so bad. I couldn't beat her any more. I knocked out all the windows. I just was a raging lunatic.

Harley elaborated on his beliefs.

> My first wife, I used to just beat her so bad, just turn the house up side down and just beat her. For what reason? She may have asked me a question, asked me, why did I go to work that day. Any kind of question that doesn't sit with me turns into violence. I could always take it and turn whatever they said into the way I wanted it to be. What are you trying to do? You're trying to shame me. You're trying to embarrass me. You're not giving me any respect. Those are my famous words: 'I'm a grown man. I deserve my respect. I want my respect. You don't come in, and you don't try to

tell me what to do.'

Besides beliefs about women, what it means to be a man, and the right to construct others as they see fit, many perpetrators also believe that if they are hurting enough they have the right to hurt others. Cory raped and beat his wife in front of their three year-old daughter because he was convinced his wife had cheated on him. Many men believe that if wives cheat, men have to punish them and re-establish themselves as men. This is how Cory described his hurt and what he does with it.

When somebody's done something or what not, I'll say to myself, I'll use my exact words. 'You fucking dickhead, you have no idea of who you're even saying that to. I'll rip your skull off.' That sense of power is inside of me. It's always there, that sense of power, how powerful you are. Okay? I go, 'Listen to you.' That will be my exact words. 'If you only knew. If you only knew.'

This is weird about me. All right? I see myself with this great big heart. Okay? Picture this. This heart in me is this big. (He holds his hands about two feet apart.) At times when somebody comes up and tries to poke that heart that I get relatively mad. Okay? Then sometimes when that heart actually gets punctured then I get angry and rageful. Okay? In most cases in my life, I think, the person that got hurt was me. There were times when I got tired of hurting me and I want somebody else to pay. Like the time I beat my wife.

Enjoyment

Like many other perpetrators, Harley enjoyed himself as he behaved in violent ways.

I actually had these people afraid. My family's afraid. The people outside my family's afraid. Friends of my family's afraid. My sister's girlfriend, her and her husband came over to the house one night. Her husband, like we got into an argument. I jumped up, and I grabbed him, slammed him up against the wall. Here's my sister crying. Here's this guy's wife--she's crying. I'm like, what are these people crying about? They're giving me this high, this, this feeling of control or power.

I got power now over these people. They're telling me, "Oh don't hurt him. Don't hurt him." My sister, she said, "You don't know my brother. Control yourself. He might kill him." I've got this power. I love that. I love people to dress me up.

Don

Almost all of the perpetrators I interviewed enjoyed themselves while they were being violent. Don, a high school football player, described the physical experience of anticipating his rapes.

> Well, nothing, nothing ever gave me the intense kind of feeling. Especially the, there would be, like, like when I was driving around and I would be thinking about it, maybe following somebody, I had, you know, like a physical reaction. I would be shaking, physically shaking, like teeth would chatter, and I couldn't stop. You know, it wouldn't stop, and I never had that kind of, you know, physical reaction to, to anything else. I would also get, you know, like butterflies and I can, you know, relate that to, you know, sports events, you know, before a big game or something. You know, that feeling but not the, not the physical [meaning, he didn't have an erection before a big game, but did when he was driving around looking for a woman alone after dark in her car].

Anticipating rape inflamed Don. His behavior evoked images of man the hunter, man the questor, man the predator, man the sports hero. This also is showing himself as a real man. For Don, the audience is himself and perhaps an imaginary audience who believed, as he told me he did, that real men have sex whenever they want. He was living up to his ideal of man the sexual conqueror who has sex with whomever he chooses whenever he wants.

Cory

Cory also enjoyed his violence. I could see that as he described what happened when somebody pricked his great big heart: "You have no idea who you're dealing with." He thought beating his wife would help him feel better about his conviction that she had cheated on him. He told me

> That night I said to myself, If you go over there and do this you're going to feel better afterwards, you know. I'm going to make you pay for hurting me. This is the last time you're going to hurt me.

In acts of physical violence with other men, his wounds were badges of manhood. He said

I've woken up in the morning with this lip hanging out here, eyes swollen shut, and my nose broken. I had my friends come over. We yucked it up about it. 'Ha, ha. That was a hell of a fight, wasn't it?' Somehow I was a man then.

Same Patterns, Different Cases

I saw these patterns repeatedly in my interviews with men who had committed violent acts: beliefs and enjoyment. In media reports of violence, these same features show up repeatedly. A few examples, some of them old, show what I mean. A witness to the school murders in Littleton, Colorado, said "every time they'd shoot someone, they'd holler, like it was, like, exciting."

Another student reported, "They were laughing after they shot. It was like they were having the time of their lives." In 1996, 14 year-old Barry Loukatis, killed a boy who had teased him. He also killed two other boys. He said "It sure beats algebra, doesn't it?' as he stood over a dying boy who was choking on his own blood. This was 16 years ago. Yet, I am unsure that these two main ideas: beliefs and enjoyment are connected to violence in people's minds.

Murder of Children in China

In the past five weeks, four men in China assaulted and killed preschool children and children in primary schools. Because guns are unavailable in China, three men used knives and one a hammer. Almost 60 children were injured and eight additional children died. Had they assailants used guns, many more children and adults would have died. In the latest attack, on the last day of April, teachers pulled two children from the attackers arms as he prepared to light himself on fire. He died in the fire.

Newspaper articles quoted Chinese citizens who can't understand why this is happening. The article also provided several theories. The men are unemployed and are taking their frustration out on children. "Children are the one people care about the most, and they are the most innocent," said a sociology professor at a Chinese university. Some speculated that these are copycat killings, given the publicity about them. Finally, there are thoughts that the men are mentally ill, which led to expressions of concerns about China's lack of mental health services.

None of these theories mentioned beliefs and none mentioned the emotional gratification the men may have experienced as they planned and then acted on their violence.

Beliefs are likely to have had a lot to do with these attacks on children. All four perpetrators were men. It is likely that they interpreted their circumstances in terms of their masculinity. The gap between what they thought they should achieve and what they actually achieved may have been impossible for them to handle. Their unemployment may have convinced them they were unworthy of respect.

They may have become alienated from friends and family rather than seeking comfort from them. Their beliefs about masculinity may have led them to believe that they would be seen as even less worthy of respect as men, as being weak, if they admitted to others how upset and hurt they were. Under no circumstances could they risk seeing themselves as weak, or having others see them that way.

Thus, they probably were hurting badly, based upon their beliefs. Like Cory, they may have wanted others to hurt as badly as they did. They may have chosen young children as victims because they knew this would hurt other people badly. Hurting adults is not as big a hurt as harming children.

They also may have felt like nobodies. When they saw other men get noticed when they harmed children may have given them ideas about how others would know who they are.

The one man who killed himself may have felt so much intense hurt—the kind of hurt that Cory described—that his only way out was to set himself on fire. His attempt to take two children with him suggests that he was dead serious about hurting others as he was hurt.

Newspaper accounts do not state what the demeanors of the men were, but based on my research, I believe that they felt their spirits lifting when they planned their crimes as they committed their crimes. Violence helped them feel better, too, just as others I've quoted and so many other cases show.

Mental illness is a popular explanation for why people commit such violent acts. This does not hold water because most people who have mental illnesses are not violent, just as most people who do not have mental illnesses are not violent. People with mental illnesses who are violent have beliefs that violence is what you are supposed to do under certain prescribed circumstances. People with mental illnesses and who are violent have the same beliefs as people without mental illness and who are violent.

Murder in Minneapolis, Minnesota, USA

After Trace Maxwell killed his girlfriend and two men, he led police on a slow chase down city streets until he shot and killed himself in late April 2010. Newspaper reports give few details about what was going on in Trace's mind. He obviously thought murder and suicide would solve whatever what bothering him. He also shot his girlfriend's roommate, but she survived.

Trace appeared to have believed his girlfriend had cheated on him. Like Cory and Harley, his solution was violence. Somehow his manhood was disrespected, and he was going to set her straight. He believed the two men had cheated him out of money. Trace was, among other things, a drug dealer and pimp who had been in prison. If he were a real man, he could not let these men get away with cheating him. His friends said he killed himself because he did not want to go back to prison.

That might be so, but down deep, he may have believed that as a grown man, no one could tell him what to do, including ordering him to prison for three murders and one attempted murder. He was going to get away with it, and he was going to be in control of his life, even if it meant ending his life.

Trace had a hair-trigger temper, often "going off" on people. His long record of police involvement shows a pattern of not controlling this emotional responses. A technical term for his "temper" is "reactivity." Trace apparently had a highly reactive way of dealing with things that displeased him. A lot of people do. Many of their highly reactive responses are related to unresolved traumas, such as abuse and neglect in childhood, witnessing violence, bullying, losses, thinking that's what you are supposed to do, and the like.

Any one or several of these factors may have been true for Trace as well. Yet, most highly reactive people do not murder others and most do not hurt others. They may hurt themselves through cutting themselves, overeating, or drinking too much alcohol, or they may deal constructively with their strong emotional reactions. Very few murder, rape, beat others up, or even verbally abuse others.

With Trace, then, the core issue is beliefs about what he is entitled to do when he is upset with others. Murder them—that is what he believed. When other people are closing in on him, don't let that happen. Kill yourself. These are beliefs.

Newspaper accounts do not have information about whether Trace felt gratified as he planned and executed his shootings and murders, but he must have. The satisfaction of doing exactly what you want is gratifying. The satisfaction of foiling police in not allowing them to take him alive must have been gratifying.

Discussion

It's time to stop wondering why they do it. They do it because they believe violence is what they are supposed to do. A web of beliefs comes together when people commit violent acts. The anticipation of gratification at committing violence and the gratification of actually doing the violence overcome any thoughts that such acts are not a good idea.

It's time to think about what each of us can do to unravel beliefs that lead to violent acts.

References

5 Chinese kids hurt in new attack (2010). *Minneapolis Star Tribune.* May 1, 2010. p. A6.

Gilgun, Jane F. (2010). *Child sexual abuse: From harsh realities to hope.* Amazon Kindle and scribd.com.

Gilgun, Jane F. (2010). *The NEATS: A child and family assessment.* Amazon Kindle, and scribd.com,

Gilgun, Jane F. (2008). Lived experience, reflexivity, and research on perpetrators of interpersonal violence. *Qualitative Social Work, 7(2),* 181-197.

Gilgun, Jane F. (1999). Fingernails painted red: A feminist, semiotic analysis of "hot" text, *Qualitative Inquiry, 5,* 181-207.

Gilgun, Jane F. (2006). Children and adolescents with problematic sexual behaviors: Lessons from research on resilience. In Robert Longo & Dave Prescott (Eds.*), Current perspectives on working with sexually aggressive youth and youth with sexual behavior problems* (pp. 383-394). Holyoke, MA: Neari Press.

Gilgun, Jane F., & Laura S. Abrams (2005). Gendered adaptations, resilience, and the perpetration of violence. In Michael Ungar (Ed.*), Handbook for working with children and Youth: Pathways to resilience across cultures and context* (pp. 57-70). Toronto: University of Toronto Press

Gilgun, Jane F., Danette Jones, & Kay Rice. (2005). Emotional expressiveness as an indicator of progress in treatment. In Martin C. Calder (Ed.), *Emerging approaches to work with children and young people who sexually abuse* (pp. 231-244). Dorset, England: Russell House.

Gilgun, Jane F., & Laura McLeod (1999). Gendering violence. *Studies in Symbolic Interactionism, 22,* 167-193.

Gilgun, Jane F. (1996). Human development and adversity in ecological perspective, Part 2: Three patterns. *Families in Society, 77,* 459-576.

Gilgun, Jane F. (1996). Human development and adversity in ecological perspective: Part 1: A conceptual framework. *Families in Society, 77,* 395-402.

Gilgun, Jane F. (1995). We shared something special: The moral discourse of incest perpetrators. *Journal of Marriage and the Family, 57,* 265-281.

McKinney, Matt, Joy Powell, & David Chanen (2010). Hints of motives appear in Twin Cities slaying rampage. *Minneapolis Star Tribune.* May 1, 2010. A1, A7.

Sharma, Alankaar & Jane F. Gilgun (2008). What perpetrators say about child sexual abuse. *Indian Journal of Social Work, 69(3),* 321-338.

14

Women's Aging Bodies
and What to Do about our Aging Parts

Reviewer: "if you want to feel old, go ahead and get the book"

Women often do not know about the changes they may experience as they grow older. This short article outlines the changes that women can expect by the time they reach 50 and beyond. I start from the top of the body and end at the feet. I talk mostly about what I have experienced myself, but I have not experienced all of the changes I mention.

There are other changes that women experience as they grow older. In this article, I have the simple purpose of wanting to let other women know about some of what they can expect as they age and to help younger women head off preventable issues related to aging. Much of this is about bodily changes. Changes in how we think, love, and expect are much deeper topics. I mention them, but much more can be said.

One general observation that I can make about bodily changes as we age is that a lot of our body parts are more dry than they used to be. For just about any change, however, there is a response that makes us more comfortable.

Hair

My hair is drier and thinner. I've always used conditioner and still do. Fortunately, I have a lot of hair and so I still have a full head of hair. Some women lose hair, and some of them use wigs or falls. Many do not. Loss of pubic hair also can happen as we get older.

I'm getting gray hair. Women have varying degrees of gray hair as they age. Some just go gray. Some dye their hair. Some have hair stylists streak their hair. Streaking disguises gray hair.

I also have a few stray hairs sprouting around my mouth and chin that I did not have when I was younger. I've had some removed through electrolysis, but others come back. I pluck them. I will have them removed permanently because I don't want random sprouts on my chin when I am too old to pull them out myself.

Brains

Many older women are wiser than they have ever been. Brains appear to change for the better over time. Balanced nutrition and exercise over the lifetime and genes are responsible for excellent brain function later in life.

There are some conditions that may be part of normal aging that have neutral and negative effects. Calcium deposits are common in older women and men. I have them. There may be one deposit or several. As of now, neurologists believe that calcium deposits have no effect on brain functions now or in the future and are not linked to dementia, Alzheimer's, or other brain diseases later on. They also are unrelated to arthritis, which is related to calcium deposits, not, apparently, to diet.

Balance is an issue for older people, possibly related to changes in brains. Thus, exercises to maintain capacities for balance can be helpful. I stand on one foot for about 20 seconds per day and walk on curbs of sidewalks to help me keep my sense of balance. Riding bikes might help, as would any form of exercise, most likely.

Body Fat

Body fat seems to thin as we get older. My derriére does not tolerate sitting on hard seats for as long as it used to. Riding my bike, however, I find that body part toughens over the season.

When I was a child, I was afraid I would get arm flaps like my beloved Aunt Jo—skin on my triceps that hung loose. I've got them, and I live with them. Some women wear tops that have three-quarter length sleeves or sleeves that extend to elbows.

Skin

Brown spots and wrinkles are part of normal aging, and I have both. Heredity and overexposure to sun appear to be the cause. Since there is melanoma in my immediate family, I go to a dermatologist for a full body check every year. For a fee, she removes the age spots from my face and everywhere else they appear. Laser treatments do something similar. I also use a prescription cream on my face that diminishes the likelihood of growing new age spots. The cream also helps prevent wrinkles, according to research.

A few age spots have been precancerous and one was pre-melanoma, a serious form of cancer. The dermatologist removed them. These precancerous spots typically are part of aging, too.

Loose skin under the chin is part of aging. I've thought I'd have plastic surgery when mine appeared. Mine has appeared, and I haven't had surgery. Maybe I will someday.

Eyes

I had my first floater when I was in my thirties, which is young to have them, but I am also near-sighted. Floaters are dark bits that jump around inside the eyes. For about a year, several years ago, I had frequent floaters and also noticed flashes of light. I went to an eye specialist to find out about the flashing lights. I knew about floaters—thickening pieces of the solution that makes up much of the eye, but the flashes were a mystery. The doctor said it was good I came in because flashes and floaters could indicate a detached retina. I did not have one, she concluded, after examining my eyes in a variety of ways. She said floaters are also related to changes in the fluid in eyes.

Most people get far sighted—can't read fine print, for example—by their forties. That didn't happen to me. I was probably near-sighted when I was born.

A few years ago, an ophthalmologist told me I have cataracts—the one in my right eye bigger than the one in my left. She said most people get cataracts as they age. I may require surgery when I can no longer read. I can still read, but the print is not as clear as it once was.

For a couple of years, my eyes hurt, and the ophthalmologist said I have dry eyes. She suggested eye drops for dry eyes. I used them for a while, but I don't seem to need them now.

Nose

Sometimes my nose seems drier than it used to be. Not lately, though. When it seems dry, I flush with saline solution, available at pharmacies.

Mouth

The dental hygienist just told me I have dry mouth. I hadn't noticed. She gave me a small bottle of mouthwash for dry mouth. I love it. I swish that mouthwash about three times a day. It's supposed to help maintain teeth and gum health by replacing enzymes that appear to diminish as we age.

Good overall care of teeth over the lifetime pays off in older ages. Flossing, brushings, and regular cleaning will help avoid teeth loss for most of us in older age. Teeth implants are a growing substitute for dentures when teeth go missing. They are expensive. Some insurance plans may cover them, but mine doesn't.

Midriff

I can usually tell when a woman has hit menopause. She gains weight. I did. I didn't realize it. The gain was gradual. What appears to happen is that we eat amounts we always have but our metabolism slows and we don't need as much food as we used to. So our bodies kindly store the food for us for later use. The solution? Eat less. I did it by making sure that I eat at least five portions of fruit and vegetables a day, several ounces of protein, some high fiber cereal that tastes good, and at least two portions of calcium rich foods such as skim milk and yoghurt. I also limit my intake of butter, sugar, and caffeine. On this diet I lost 15 pounds without even trying.

Intestines

I ate a lot of cashews one evening. They tasted so good to me. The next day, I had incredible pain in my left side. I phoned the doctor, who got me in right away. She took a history, did an exam, and said I had eaten too many cashews. I did not have a perforated intestine. She said the part of the intestine that connects the large intestine to the small does not work as effectively as we age. It simply can't handle that many nuts. I said I gotten milder pain when I eat a lot of beef and lamb. She said the same reason.

I still eat too much fiber sometime, as I did this morning. I drank three glasses of water. That seems to help the pain, moves things along, so to speak.

Many older people have problems with constipation. Even eating a lot of fiber from fruits, vegetables, and grains doesn't seem not to help. There are daily fiber doses you can buy and that might help. For a small number of older people, constipation is a way of life.

Colonoscopies can detect early stages of cancer and pre-cancer. These procedures are not fun, but they are important. Persons with family histories of rectal-colon cancer should have colonoscopies more regularly than those without these histories.

Bladder

Many women develop pushy bladders when they get older. What seems to happen is that aging affects muscle tone. When we urinate, we exercise expulsion muscles, while the retaining muscles soften. So, when we have an impulse to expel, the retaining muscles are weaker than expulsion muscles. When we gotta go, we gotta—that's the result. So, we have to figure out how to strengthen the retention muscles. I strengthen my muscles most days while in the shower. I pull in my abs and pull up at the same time. Works wonders. There's more information on the Internet.

Vagina

Many women experience dryness in vaginal tissue that can result in painful intercourse and itching. This results from thinning of tissue connected to the body's production of less estrogen. Estrogen creams can be a great help. Sometimes doctors prescribe a steroid that can help with itching. Sometimes odor becomes a problem in older age. Compounds that contain boric acid, which neutralizes some of the odors.

Knees, Hips, & Other Joints

Many older people have pain in their joints. This can be arthritis. Much of the pain is from wear and tear and old sports injuries. Some is related to heredity, and some might be related to poor nutrition in childhood. Doctors can be of great help for this kind of pain. Hip and knee surgery and replacements are less hard on the body than they used to be and almost everyone who has the surgery does much better afterward.

I've had to wear expensive, well-made shoes since I was in my early forties because with thin-soled shoes, both my ankles hurt. I broke my right ankle once and sprained it three times. That could explain pain in that ankle, but I had not injured the left ankle and the pain is the same when I'm not careful about footwear. So, I must have some sort of hereditary condition.

Bones

Thinning of the bones is common in older women and some men. Heredity and nutrition appear to be major reasons. Today's young women know to exercise, eat plenty of calcium-rich foods, and to avoid smoking. Many women my age and years younger did not grow up knowing this. Many have thin bones, either osteoporosis or osteopenia, which is a milder form of bone loss.

Medication, judicious exercise, and a nutritious diet can help women with osteopenia, as can taking calcium pills with vitamin D and spending time in the sun. Prevention of osteoporosis and osteopenia requires the same diet, exercise, and sun exposure.

Muscles and Tendons

We probably stiffen as we grow older. I've been stretching in the shower for decades and lift small weights. After all of these years, I can almost touch my toes. I've actually I think most medical people agree that stretching and weights are important to build or maintain muscle tone and flexibility. I took many lessons about how to do this safely.

There are many kinds of other exercises such as yoga, dancing, and tai chi, that help with muscle tone and tendons. They also help relax us.

Loss

By the time we've hit our fifties, we've experienced many losses and have many more to come. Maintaining a sense of optimism may take a lot more work than it did when we were younger. I've found that journaling and vigorous exercise are a great help. Some people benefit from support groups, therapy, and counseling. Whatever it takes. Optimism and purpose are key to meaningful lives. Medical consultation helps some people find direction after loss.

Thinking, Expecting, Loving

Growing older is not much fun when I think that I can now envision the end of my life. It's also not much fun when I think that there may come a time when I can no longer ride my horses. It's also not much fun when someone calls me "young lady."

When I suspect that younger people are put off by my age, I can sympathize and realize that they have not yet come to terms with the fact of their own aging. They will be here before they know it, if they are lucky.

I've heard many people a lot older than me say that in their hearts and minds they are still young. The person who looks back at them in the mirror is not the person they are inside.

I know what they mean. I still have many expectations for my life. I love what I have always loved and look forward to new loves. I think I'm thinking as well as I ever had, although a bank teller yesterday kidded me when I made a math error, an error in my checking account number, and put the wrong date on the deposit slip. I might have done that when I was younger. I wanted to tell him I am a professor, and professors are absent-minded, but I thought I had better not substitute that stereotype for whatever the young man might have been thinking. I laughed about these errors. You know what? I actually did think they were funny and felt no shame at all.

That's probably the best part of aging. Who cares about silly things? Of course I make mistakes. So what? The grass is still green in the summer. The flowers still bloom in the spring. The birds still sing in the trees. So much to celebrate and to love. Growing older may help us understand what matters.

Note: This brief article is based primarily on my personal experience and is not intended as a substitute for expert medical advice.

\

ABOUT THE AUTHOR

Jane Gilgun, PhD, LICSW, is a professor, School of Social Work, University of Minnesota, Twin Cities, USA. See Jane's other books, articles, and children's stories on Amazon, iBooks, Barnes & Noble, and Kobo. She enjoys Ireland, horses, gardening, writing, the arts, boating, and cooking.